THE MIDDLE SCHOOL MATHEMATICIAN

Empowering Students to Achieve Success in Algebra and Geometry

by Terri Breeden
and
Kathryn Dillard

Incentive Publications, Inc.
Nashville, Tennessee

Illustrated by Kathleen Bullock
Cover by Geoffrey Brittingham
Edited by Leslie Britt

ISBN 0-86530-330-4

2 3 4 5 6 7 8 9 10 07 06

PRINTED IN THE UNITED STATES OF AMERICA
www.incentivepublications.com

Table of Contents

Part Three: Geometry Readiness

Resources and References

About This Book

The middle school mathematics curriculum has changed in the last few years. With the publication of the *National Council of Teachers of Mathematics (NCTM) Standards,* math teaching techniques have begun to evolve. Basic skill drills are receiving less emphasis while technology and problem-solving strategies are receiving more emphasis. The NCTM organization has stated that algebra concepts be integrated into the mathematics curriculum, from kindergarten through the twelfth grade. Further insight was gained when the publication *Changing the Odds* stated that students who successfully complete high school geometry increase the probability that they will attend and complete college.

How can *The Middle School Mathematician* help the middle school teacher? Since the teacher continues to be accountable for standardized test scores, this book begins with a terrific new way to review rational numbers. These activities are geared to the active nature of middle school students. Puzzles, games, and cooperative learning activities are presented. They may be used as review activities, lesson starters, or simply to enhance a specific lesson.

The second portion of the book was specifically designed to incorporate algebra concepts into the middle school curriculum. While any middle grade teacher will enjoy completing these activities with his or her students, it is an invaluable resource for the middle school teacher who teaches a seventh or eighth grade introductory algebra class. Learning how to work with integers, expressions, and equations in middle school has a huge impact on future mathematical success. The authors are experienced middle school educators who have used all of these readiness activities with their own middle school students.

The final chapter of the book focuses on geometry. The activities were designed to help students develop their spatial abilities and their understanding of polygons, lines, angles, and symmetry. Students will also receive an introduction to tessellations and fractals. These two topics are especially popular among students in the middle grades.

The authors realize the amount of time it takes for teachers to develop games and activities for a classroom and have created this book so that the busy teacher (with access to a photocopy machine, index cards, and scissors) can use these activities immediately. After copying the activity or making a few cards, the teacher is ready to incorporate into any existing math curriculum challenging activities that are in line with the NCTM Standards.

Part One:
Getting In Shape With Rational Numbers

SHADY NUMBERS

Numbers . . . they are shady characters. You have to keep an eye on them!

In the grid below, a secret message is hidden from your view. If you shade in all of the "shady" odd numerals, you will be able to decode the message!

18	3	16	14	26	48	24	88	46	72	92
5	2	17	28	30	98	5	50	86	90	47
13	20	23	4	24	52	3	20	10	66	13
9	32	27	40	6	100	39	54	30	56	1
7	22	11	12	97	33	43	44	73	81	65
25	34	29	42	95	8	35	60	15	58	89
21	38	19	10	93	62	37	402	397	60	87
36	15	46	44	99	29	41	40	401	77	143

Name ______________________________ Date ____________

APART BINGO

Fractions are easy to learn if you first understand their meaning. Below is an APART Bingo game mat with squares divided into either halves, thirds, or fourths.

To Play:

1. Color fractional portions of each box to construct your own personalized Bingo game mat. Don't forget to leave some fraction boxes uncolored to represent zero. It might even help you to win if you include a fraction that equals a whole.
2. After you have constructed your game mat, form a cooperative group with at least two other students. Cut out the APART cards and markers (page 11) and place them in a stack.
3. Each player takes turns drawing an APART card from the stack. When a player draws a card which matches a box with that fractional portion colored, he or she places an APART marker on that box. (Only one box can be covered each turn.) The first player to have five markers in a row is the winner.

Name ______________________________ Date ____________

APART BINGO CARDS

0/2	1/2	2/2	0/2	1/2
2/2	0/3	1/3	2/3	3/3
0/3	1/3	2/3	3/3	0/4
1/4	2/4	3/4	4/4	0/4
1/4	2/4	3/4	4/4	Free

APART APART APART APART APART APART APART APART

APART APART APART APART APART APART APART APART

APART APART APART APART APART APART APART APART

APART APART APART APART APART APART APART APART

FRACTION EMPIRE

Enter the medieval age as a courageous Knight. Your mission is to conquer equivalent fractions in order to build your own empire. Only two Knights can enter the battle arena at one time.

You will need the following materials:

• Two dice • One Fraction Empire game board (page 13) • A pencil

To Play:

1. Knights take turns rolling both dice to determine their fraction. For example, Knight One rolls a 2 and a 3.
2. The numbers are stated as a fraction, no greater than 1. Knight One would say, "Two-thirds."
3. The first Knight then initials two-thirds of a Fraction Empire Circle on the game board. For example, Knight One could initial two slices from the circle with three slices, four slices from the circle with six slices, six slices from the circle with nine slices, or eight slices from the circle with twelve slices.
4. If a Knight rolls a value of 1, such as a 3 and a 3 (three-thirds), the Knight rolls again.
5. Knight Two follows the same procedure and initials his or her Fraction Empire Slices on the same game board.
6. The game ends when all of the Fraction Empire Slices have been initialed or when time has expired.
7. The winner is the Knight whose conquered (initialed) slices total the greatest value. Each Knight must add the value of all of his or her initialed slices. Each Knight should then check the other Knight's work.

FRACTION EMPIRE

Divisibility Dash
(a game for 2 to 4 players)

Construct the spinner below by cutting out the spinner base, the washer and the pointer. Using a single hole punch, place a hole in the center of both the washer and the pointer. Order the pieces of the spinner in the following manner: spinner base (bottom); washer (middle); pointer (top). Secure all three pieces with a small brad. Spin the spinner several times to make sure that it turns smoothly. Adjust the brad if the spinner does not move smoothly and evenly.

To Play:

1. Each player places a marker on the Start box of the game board (page 15). Each player turns the spinner. The player who lands on the lowest number plays first.
2. The first player spins and moves the number of spaces indicated by the spinner. If a clue is given, the player moves accordingly.
3. The object of the game is to be the first player to reach Finish. If two players land on the same space, the player who landed on the space first is sent back to start. To win, a player must spin a number that places him or her exactly on the Finish box. For example, if the player is two spaces from Finish, the player must spin a two to win. If the player spins a three, he or she can move the two spaces to Finish and then turn back to land on one space away from the Finish box.

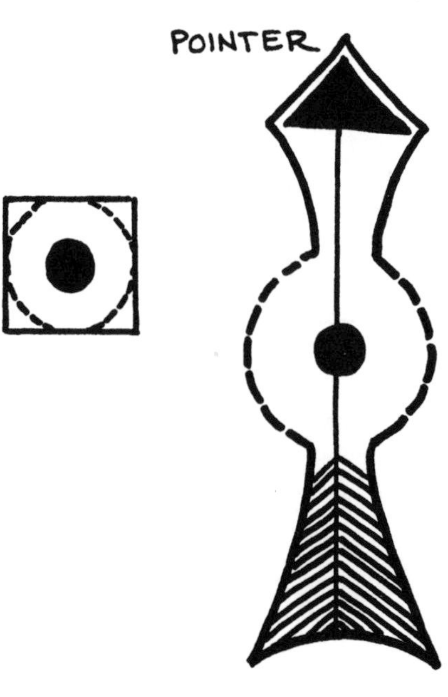

Divisibility Dash

START

- You know that all even numbers are divisible by 2. Move forward 2 spaces.
- You think that 16 is divisible by 3. Return to START.
- You know that 25 is divisible by 5. Rest here.
- You think that 27 is divisible by 4. Move back 1 space.
- If 36 and 24 are divisible by 6, then move forward 1 space.
- You failed a divisibility test! Go back 3 spaces.
- Move forward 2 spaces by naming 2 numbers divisible by 3.
- You are confused. You think that 65 is divisible by 10. Go back 3 spaces.
- If you can say the divisibility rule for 3, then advance 3 spaces.
- Go back 2 spaces. You forgot that 50 is divisible by 2, 5, and 10.
- You are a Math Whiz! You know that 60 is divisible by 2, 3,5, 6 and 10. Go forward 2 spaces.
- You made '80' on a divisibility quiz! Rest here.
- You can't remember that all numbers that end in '0' are divisible by 10. Go back 2 spaces.
- If you know the divisibility rule for 4, move ahead 3 spaces.
- You say 29 is divisible by 3! Go back 4 spaces.
- If 228 is divisible by 4, move ahead 1 space.
- Bad day in Math Class. You said 100 is divisible by 3. Go back 2 spaces.
- You say that 15, 30, and 40 are divisible by 15. Go back 3 spaces.

FINISH

Snappy Factors

Factoring is an important concept in basic algebra. This activity will help students understand and work with the principles of factoring.

The object of the activity is to find two factors that have a specified product when multiplied and have a specified sum when added. If you give them the following clues, they will find factoring to be a snap!

My product is 36.	My sum is 15.
What sets of two numbers have a **product** of 36? 1 and 36, 2 and 18, 3 and 12, 4 and 9, 6 and 6	Which of the pairs of factors have a **sum** of 15? **Only** 3 and 12

The two factors that fit both situations are 3 and 12.

In factoring, four cases exist: Positive Product /Positive Sum
Positive Product /Negative Sum
Negative Product /Positive Sum
Negative Product /Negative Sum

Materials:

- Use the sets of numbers on page 17 and the patterns on page 18 to create three sets of flash cards.
- Die
- Hundred Number game board (page 37)

To Play:

1. Divide the class into two teams, or place students in groups of two.
2. Using one set of flash cards at a time, a student shuffles the cards and places them face up.
3. Alternating turns, each player identifies what the factors must be in order for the product and sum to be correct. If the factors are identified correctly, the player rolls a die to determine the number of spaces he or she will move on the Hundred Number game board. If a player rolls a . . .
    1, advance one space and roll again.
    2, advance to the next even number.
    3, move back three spaces.
    4, move to the next multiple of four.
    5, divide your position by five and advance the number of spaces indicated by the remainder.
    6, divide your position by six and move back the number of spaces indicated by the remainder.

The first player to reach 100 wins the game.

Snappy Factors

The following sets of numbers are to be written on the Snappy Turtle patterns on page 18.

Set One: Product Is Positive Sum Is Positive		**Set Two:** Product Is Positive Sum Is Negative		**Set Three:** Product Is Negative Sum Is Positive or Negative	
PRODUCT	**SUM**	**PRODUCT**	**SUM**	**PRODUCT**	**SUM**
36	12	40	–13	–14	5
18	11	10	–7	–8	2
12	8	49	–14	–5	–4
15	16	12	–8	–6	1
36	13	5	–6	–40	–3
6	5	2	–3	–10	–3
8	9	6	–5	–24	5
9	10	1	–2	–16	–6
18	9	14	–9	–56	1
12	7	28	–11	–12	–4
15	8	12	–7	–33	8
6	7	30	–11	–24	–5
9	6	33	–14	–16	6
18	19	27	–12	–63	–2
8	6	24	–11	–15	2
40	13	10	–11	–30	1
12	13	18	–9	–20	1
20	9	4	–4	–35	2
21	10	24	–10	–24	–2
24	11	20	–9	–32	–4
30	13	16	–10	–12	–4
14	9	15	–8	–6	–1
24	10	18	–11	–7	–6
42	13	9	–6	–21	4
20	12	15	–16	–7	6
27	12	7	–8	–15	–2
63	24	9	–10	–28	3
44	24	13	–14	–32	4
72	18	23	–24	–28	12
23	24	51	–20	–64	12
75	28	57	–22		
35	12	29	–30		

SUM
PRODUCT
Snappy
SUM
PRODUCT
Snappy
SUM
PRODUCT
Snappy

THANKS, EUCLID!

Are you having trouble finding the Least Common Multiple? Never fear. Algebra and Euclid (yoo'–klid) are here! Algebra will be a big help to you in this situation. The Greek mathematician Euclid, who lived during the 3rd century B.C., documented an algebraic method for finding the Least Common Multiple (LCM) of two numbers.

Euclid found that the LCM of the variables m and n is given by the expression $\frac{m \bullet n}{g}$

The variables m and n represent your two numbers. For example, let m = 24 and n = 36. The variable g is the Greatest Common Factor (GCF) of the two numbers. In this example, the GCF of 24 and 36 is 12. Let's plug these numbers into Euclid's expression.

$$\frac{m \bullet n}{g} \qquad \frac{24 \bullet 36}{12} = \frac{864}{12} = 72$$

72 is the LCM of 24 and 36.

Find the LCM of the following numbers:

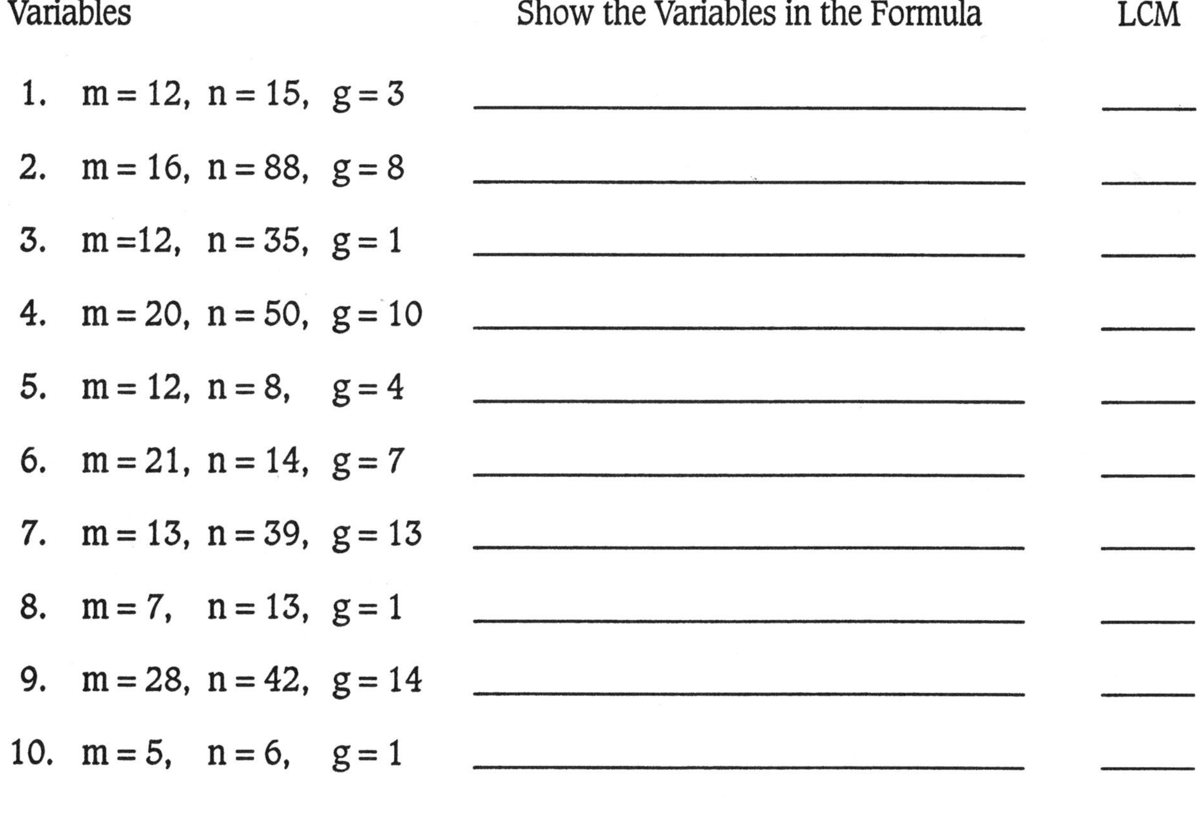

Variables	Show the Variables in the Formula	LCM
1. m = 12, n = 15, g = 3	______________________	_____
2. m = 16, n = 88, g = 8	______________________	_____
3. m =12, n = 35, g = 1	______________________	_____
4. m = 20, n = 50, g = 10	______________________	_____
5. m = 12, n = 8, g = 4	______________________	_____
6. m = 21, n = 14, g = 7	______________________	_____
7. m = 13, n = 39, g = 13	______________________	_____
8. m = 7, n = 13, g = 1	______________________	_____
9. m = 28, n = 42, g = 14	______________________	_____
10. m = 5, n = 6, g = 1	______________________	_____

Name ______________________________ Date ______________

People Hunt

Wanted . . . Students Who Can Solve Fraction Problems!

After your teacher gives you the signal, you are going on a hunt to look for students who can solve addition problems containing fractions. As quickly as you can, find people who can solve the following problems. Each participant must write the answer on the first blank and sign his or her name on the second blank.

You must have a different signature on each blank. You cannot answer any of the problems on your own sheet.

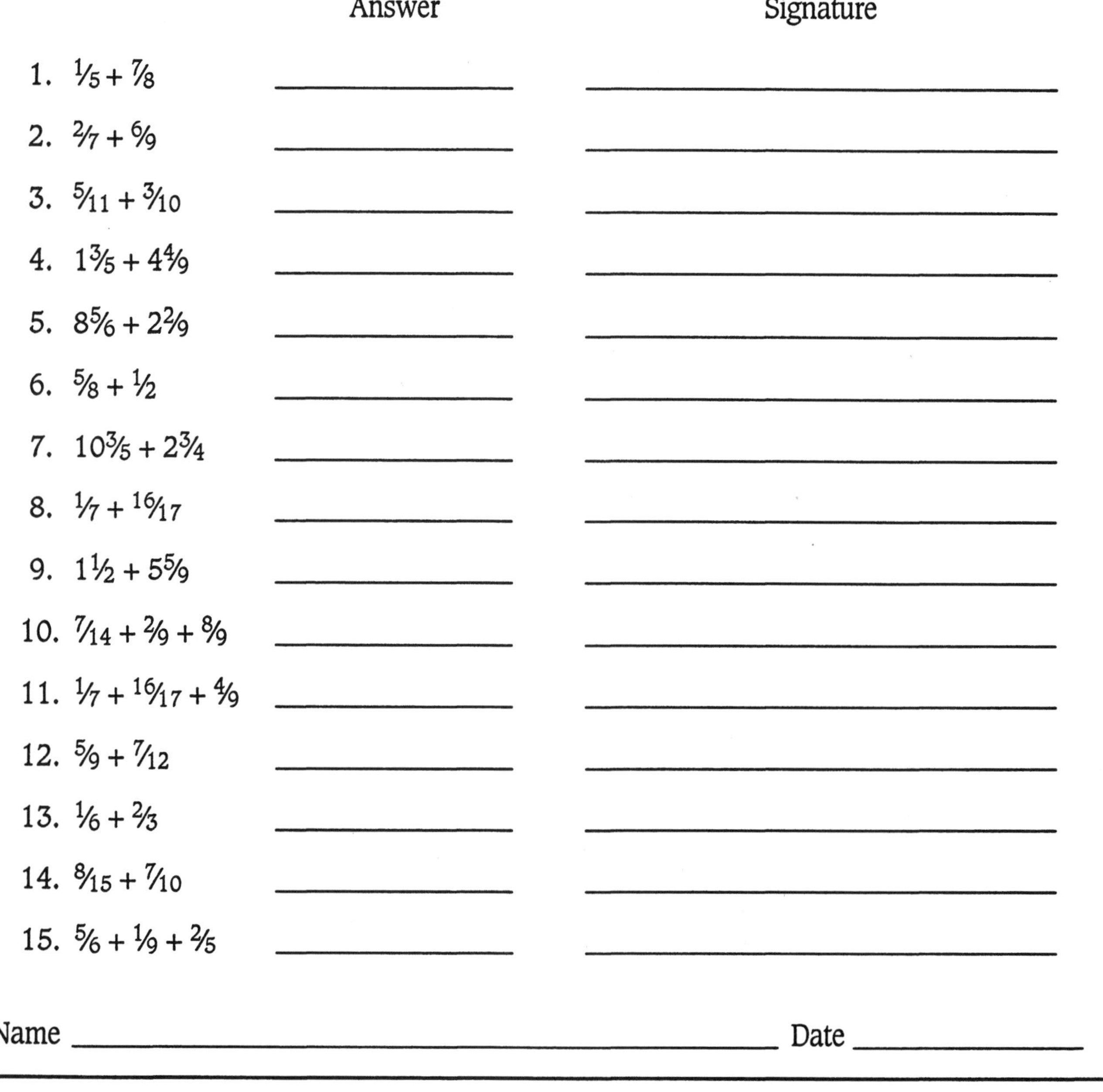

	Answer	Signature
1. $\frac{1}{5} + \frac{7}{8}$	__________	________________
2. $\frac{2}{7} + \frac{6}{9}$	__________	________________
3. $\frac{5}{11} + \frac{3}{10}$	__________	________________
4. $1\frac{3}{5} + 4\frac{4}{9}$	__________	________________
5. $8\frac{5}{6} + 2\frac{2}{9}$	__________	________________
6. $\frac{5}{8} + \frac{1}{2}$	__________	________________
7. $10\frac{3}{5} + 2\frac{3}{4}$	__________	________________
8. $\frac{1}{7} + \frac{16}{17}$	__________	________________
9. $1\frac{1}{2} + 5\frac{5}{9}$	__________	________________
10. $\frac{7}{14} + \frac{2}{9} + \frac{8}{9}$	__________	________________
11. $\frac{1}{7} + \frac{16}{17} + \frac{4}{9}$	__________	________________
12. $\frac{5}{9} + \frac{7}{12}$	__________	________________
13. $\frac{1}{6} + \frac{2}{3}$	__________	________________
14. $\frac{8}{15} + \frac{7}{10}$	__________	________________
15. $\frac{5}{6} + \frac{1}{9} + \frac{2}{5}$	__________	________________

Name ____________________________ Date __________

FRACTION DOMINOES

On heavy paper (index stock, file folders) make copies of all 28 Fraction Dominoes (page 22). Each group of 2 to 4 students will need a set of dominoes.

To Play:

1. Turn all Fraction Dominoes face down on the table. Each player draws five Fraction Dominoes and places them where the other players cannot see them. Each student should solve the fraction problems on the dominoes. The remaining dominoes are left, face down, in a draw pile. The player who draws the highest double domino (equivalent fractions, when solved) places it in the center of the table to begin. If no double is drawn, all dominoes are returned to the pile, reshuffled, and drawn again. Play moves to the left.
2. The second player tries to match one of his or her dominoes to one end of the double. For example, if a "double five" domino ($^{10}/_2$: $3\frac{1}{3} + 1\frac{2}{3}$) is the first domino played, the second player may add any domino with the value of five to one end. The next player may match the "double five" or try to match the end of the second domino played. Blank dominoes match blank dominoes. Only one domino may be played per turn. Dominoes are placed lengthwise, end to end, except in the case of doubles as shown in the example below.

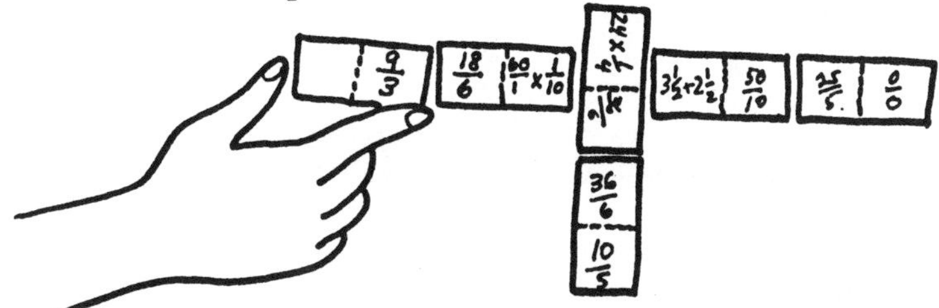

3. If a player cannot match any open end of a row, the player must pick a domino from the draw pile (this is sometimes called the Bone Yard) until able to do so. Should the last domino be drawn with no play possible, the player passes and tries again on the next turn. A player must play a domino if able to do so. Doubles are always placed at right angles, thereby giving two new directions for continued play.
4. Play continues until one player has used all of his or her dominoes or until no one can play. The player with no dominoes or with the fewest number of points (the total of the sum of the fractions on the remaining dominoes) wins the round. The winner subtracts the total of his or her remaining points (if any) from the total of the opponents' points and scores the balance from each. Rounds continue until one player scores 100 points and wins the game.

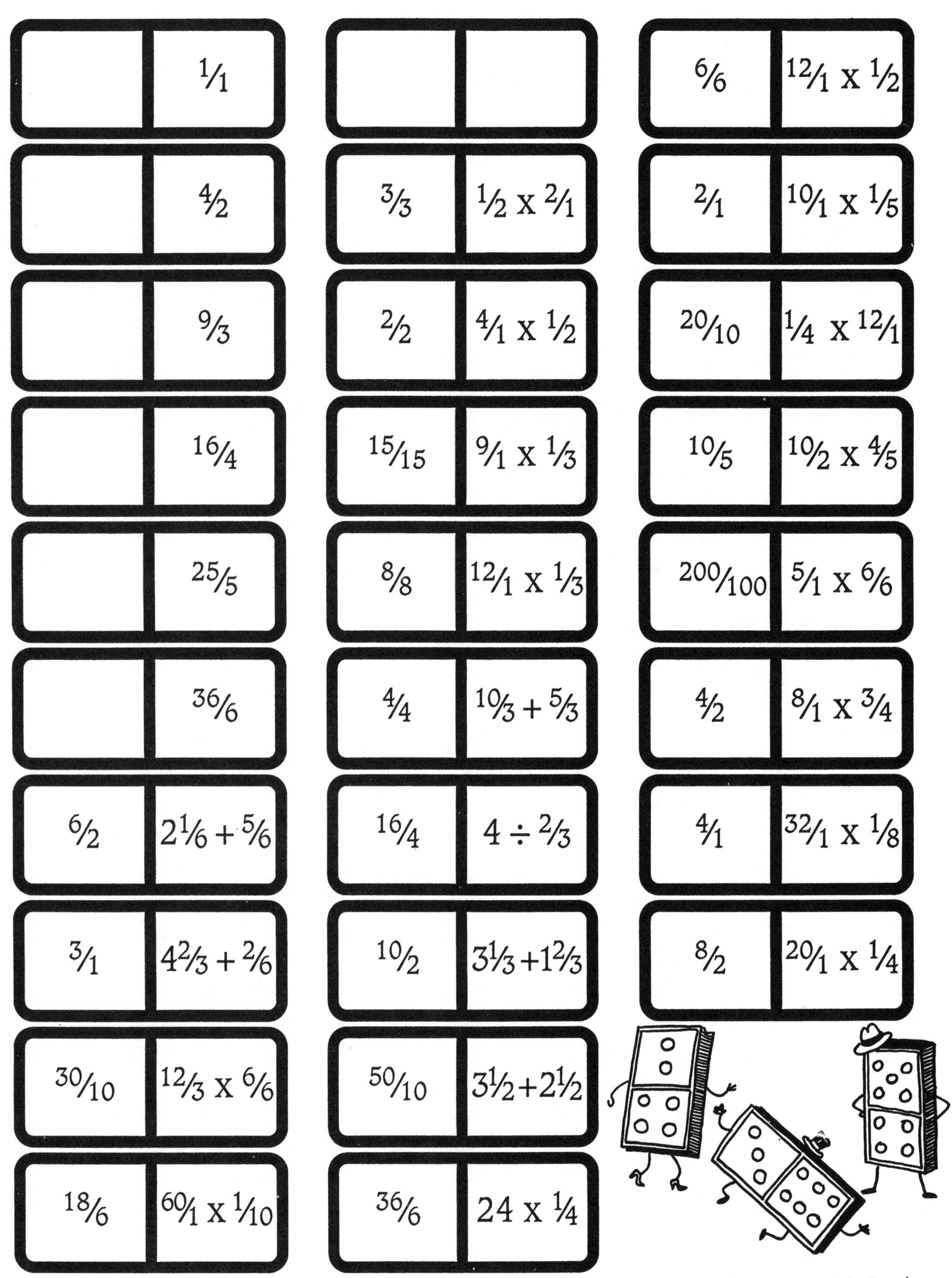

1/1
4/2
9/3
16/4
25/5
36/6
6/2 | 2 1/6 + 5/6
3/1 | 4 2/3 + 2/6
30/10 | 12/3 x 6/6
18/6 | 60/1 x 1/10
3/3 | 1/2 x 2/1
2/2 | 4/1 x 1/2
15/15 | 9/1 x 1/3
8/8 | 12/1 x 1/3
4/4 | 10/3 + 5/3
16/4 | 4 ÷ 2/3
10/2 | 3 1/3 + 1 2/3
50/10 | 3 1/2 + 2 1/2
36/6 | 24 x 1/4
6/6 | 12/1 x 1/2
2/1 | 10/1 x 1/5
20/10 | 1/4 x 12/1
10/5 | 10/2 x 4/5
200/100 | 5/1 x 6/6
4/2 | 8/1 x 3/4
4/1 | 32/1 x 1/8
8/2 | 20/1 x 1/4

True Or False Fraction Equations

In the equations below, the numbers will be represented by the following symbols:

3 = △ 2 = ○

5 = □ 9 = ◟

By substitution, determine if the equations are true or false. (Circle the word True or False.) On a separate sheet of paper, write three true equations of your own using the symbols.

1. 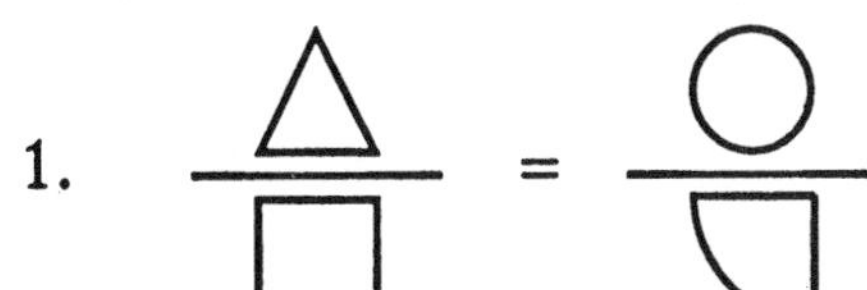 True or False

2. True or False

3. True or False

4. True or False

5. 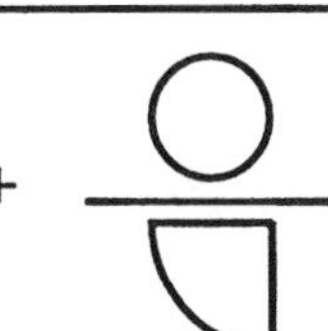 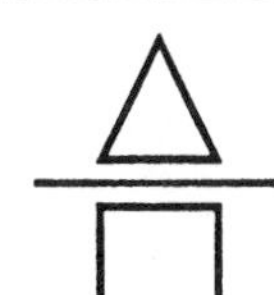  True or False

6.   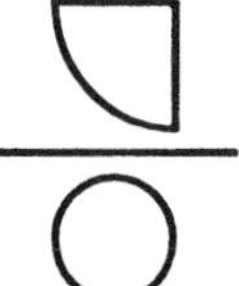 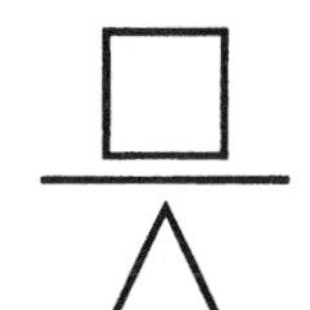  True or False

7. 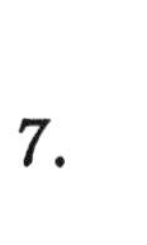 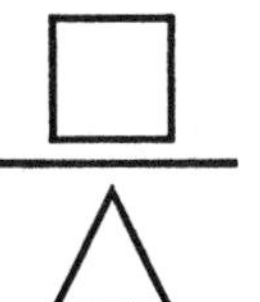 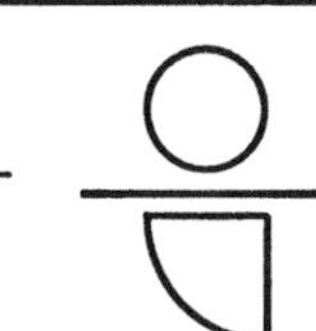 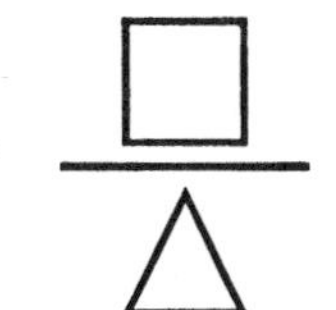 True or False

Name ______________________________ Date ______________

A Rational Crossword Puzzle

Solve the crossword puzzle below using what you know about rational numbers.

Across

1. $4/5 \times 5/4 =$______.
3. One year is what fractional part of a decade?
5. One-fourth of a dollar is a(n)______.
7. $6/12 =$ __ $/18$.
8. $5/6 \times 2\,2/5 =$_____.
9. $3/9$ can be reduced to one ______.
11. The GCF of 10 and 20 is________.
12. What number does not have a reciprocal?
14. A numeral that consists of a whole number and a fraction is a(n)________.

Down

2. $16/18$ is ____________ to $8/9$.
3. $1/2 \times 1/2 =$____________.
4. The LCM of 10 and 20 is ___.
6. $2/3$ is the __________ of $3/2$.
9. $750/2500$ can be reduced to $3/$___.
10. $z - 9/10 = 1/10$, $z =$ _________.
13. $4/5 \times 7\,1/2 =$ __________.

Name ______________________ Date __________

Name Those Numbers

Reproduce and cut apart the sets of cards on page 26. Keep each of the six sets separate. Each set of cards contains six clues about a set of two numbers.

Place the students in groups of three. Two students will challenge each other to a game of "Name Those Numbers." The third student will serve as the game host.

To Play:

1. One set of the clues is given to the host. The host asks Player 1 how many of the six clues he or she needs to "Name Those Numbers." Player 1 can choose between one and three clues initially. The host then reads the number of clues Player 1 has requested. The order in which the clues are read is not important.
2. When the host has finished reading the clues, Player 1 must name the two numbers. If Player 1 is correct, he or she receives 100 points. If Player 1 is incorrect, Player 2 may try to supply the answer. If Player 2 can name the numbers, he or she is awarded 100 points. If not, another clue is read. If either player can "Name Those Numbers" at this time, 75 points are awarded. If the numbers are still un-named, another clue can be read for a chance to receive 50 points. If clues still remain, a final chance can be taken for 25 points. If no one has guessed the correct numbers, and there are no clues left to be read, the host reveals the numbers to the players.
3. The host continues the game using another set of clues. During this round, Player 2 states how many clues he or she would like. Play continues in this fashion until all six sets of the clues are used.

Clue Cards

Name Those Numbers **Set 1** We are both even numbers.	**Name Those Numbers** **Set 3** We are both prime numbers.	**Name Those Numbers** **Set 5** Square one of us and get the other.
Name Those Numbers **Set 1** Our least common multiple is 24.	**Name Those Numbers** **Set 3** We are both less than 25.	**Name Those Numbers** **Set 5** Our greatest common factor is 8.
Name Those Numbers **Set 1** Our greatest common factor is 12.	**Name Those Numbers** **Set 3** Our least common multiple is 77.	**Name Those Numbers** **Set 5** Our least common multiple is 64.
Name Those Numbers **Set 1** We are both less than 50.	**Name Those Numbers** **Set 3** Our greatest common factor is 1.	**Name Those Numbers** **Set 5** We are both divisible by 2, 4, and 8.
Name Those Numbers **Set 1** We are both divisible by 3 and 6.	**Name Those Numbers** **Set 3** Gamblers think we are lucky!	**Name Those Numbers** **Set 5** Our sum is 72.
Name Those Numbers **Set 1** Neither of us is divisible by 9.	**Name Those Numbers** **Set 3** The difference between us is 4.	**Name Those Numbers** **Set 5** Our difference is 56.
Name Those Numbers **Set 2** We are not prime or composite.	**Name Those Numbers** **Set 4** We are both even numbers.	**Name Those Numbers** **Set 6** One of us is prime and one of us is composite.
Name Those Numbers **Set 2** We are consecutive digits.	**Name Those Numbers** **Set 4** We are ≤ 100.	**Name Those Numbers** **Set 6** One of us is two times the other.
Name Those Numbers **Set 2** We are ≤ 1.	**Name Those Numbers** **Set 4** Our greatest common factor is 2.	**Name Those Numbers** **Set 6** Our greatest common factor is 5.
Name Those Numbers • Set 2 You can divide one of us by the other, but if you divide by the other one, the result is undefined.	**Name Those Numbers** **Set 4** Our least common multiple is 4,900.	**Name Those Numbers** **Set 6** Our least common multiple is 10.
Name Those Numbers **Set 2** When we are squared, we don't change a bit!	**Name Those Numbers** **Set 4** The difference between us is 2.	**Name Those Numbers** **Set 6** Our product is 50. We are ≤ 20.
Name Those Numbers **Set 2** The larger number minus the smaller number is equal to the larger number.	**Name Those Numbers** **Set 4** We are consecutive even numbers.	**Name Those Numbers** **Set 6** Our quotient is either 2 or its reciprocal.

Decimals With A Touch Of Algebra

At this point in your math career, you should have a good understanding of adding and subtracting decimal numbers. Now, let's throw in some algebra.

Try to solve these algebra equations. Record your answers on a separate sheet of paper.

Example One:

3.6 + 4.9 = K
8.5 = K

Example Two:

S – 5.8 = 14.3
S – 5.8 + 5.8 = 14.3 + 5.8
S = 20.1

Example Three:

0.5 + x = 2.72
0.5 - 0.5 + x = 2.72 - 0.5
x = 2.22

1. x + 1.4 = 11.2
2. x – 1.3 =12
3. 0.32 = w – 0.1
4. s – 0.4 = 6
5. 2.34 + 1.22 = p
6. 6.01 – 3.12 = t
7. 3.6 = h – 12.7
8. y = 37 – 15.3
9. 1.2 = p – 2.7
10. 3.5 = 1.9 + b
11. 6.25 – 2.48 = u
12. k – 2.0 = 5.5
13. d = 6.34 – 2.96
14. 30 + g = 55.2
15. x = 5.8 + 8.9
16. 45.8 – x = 44.9
17. 39.6 = 22.3 + g
18. 45.32 + j = 65.9
19. 1.2 + g = 4.7
20. 23.98 + 56.8 = h
21. 86 + 6.06 = f
22. d = 5.3 + 32.8
23. g – 7.8 = 10
24. 56.9 – r = 43.1
25. 0.92 + k = 1.0

Decimal Multiplication Marathon

You and a partner are about to run the Decimal Multiplication Marathon. From the Warm Up Bank, Runner 1 selects two numbers. Cross out the two numbers selected. (You can use each number only one time.) Use a calculator to multiply the two numbers and determine the location of the product on the Distance Card. Record on your point sheet the distance you ran.

Player 2 repeats the process. When all of the numbers are crossed out, the winner is the runner who ran the farthest.

Warm Up Bank

2.7	0.7	0.128	15.4	5.97	18.4	0.05	0.992	93.1	33.5	111.1	0.6
10.3	121.5	26.3	0.03	6.43	0.76	2.4	68.01	4.2	3.44	43.1	2.09

Distance Card

If your product is between . . .

0.0–0.1	you ran	0.1 km
0.1–1.0	you ran	0.2 km
1.0–10.0	you ran	0.3 km
10.0–100.0	you ran	0.4 km
100.0–1,000.0	you ran	0.5 km
1,000.0+	you ran	too far—no points

Point Sheet

Runner 1	Runner 2
1. ______________________	1. ______________________
2. ______________________	2. ______________________
3. ______________________	3. ______________________
4. ______________________	4. ______________________
5. ______________________	5. ______________________
6. ______________________	6. ______________________
Total Distance______________	Total Distance ______________

Name ________________________________ Date ____________

Decimal Vowels

Vowels from the alphabet have been shaded on hundred-square blocks.

For example, to form the letter Y, 21 out of 100 squares have been shaded. To express the number of shaded squares to unshaded squares, we could say "twenty-one hundredths" (21/100) or "0.21" or "21 percent" of the squares are shaded.

Find the value of the other shaded vowels.

Example:

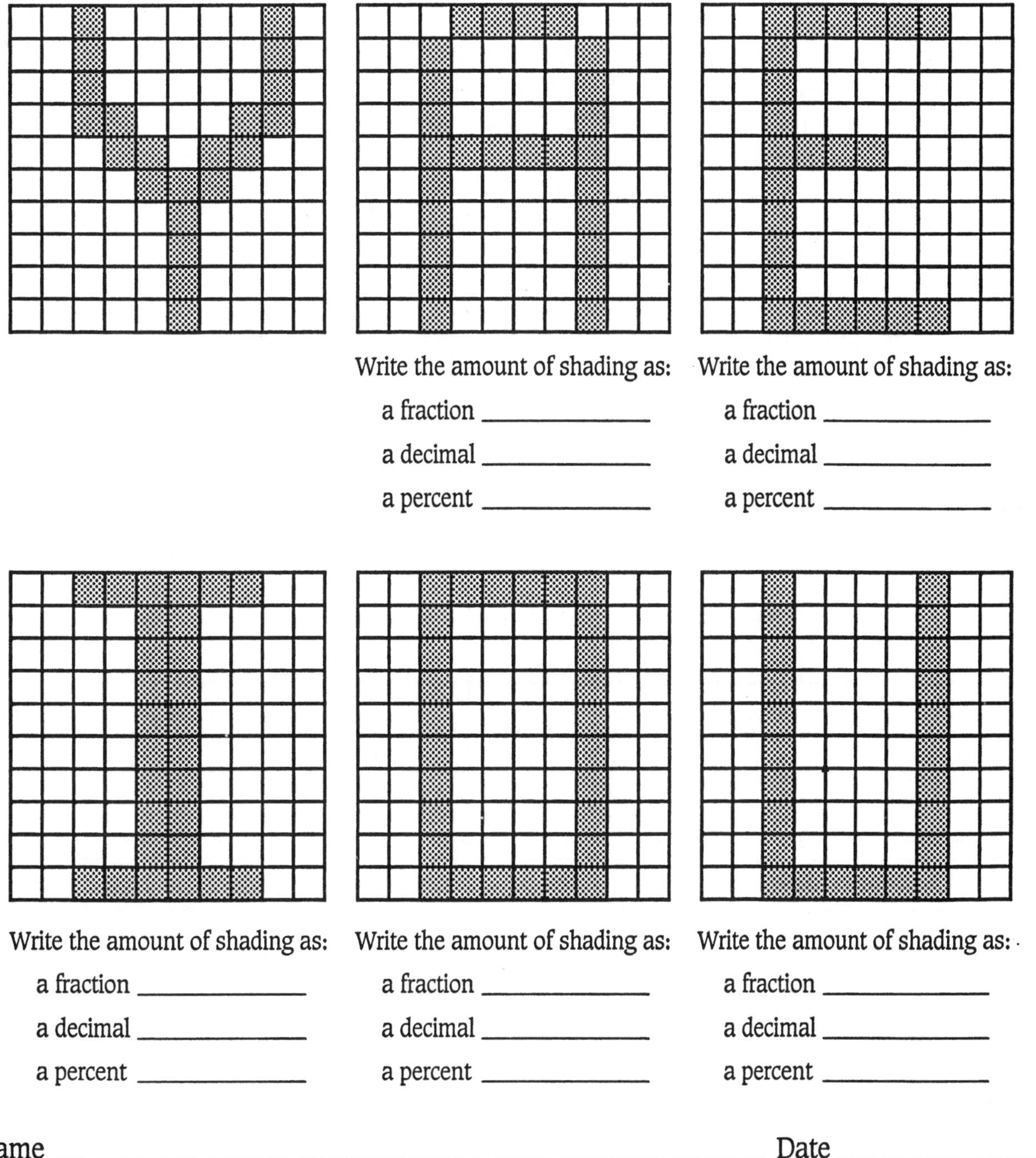

Write the amount of shading as:
a fraction ____________
a decimal ____________
a percent ____________

Write the amount of shading as:
a fraction ____________
a decimal ____________
a percent ____________

Write the amount of shading as:
a fraction ____________
a decimal ____________
a percent ____________

Write the amount of shading as:
a fraction ____________
a decimal ____________
a percent ____________

Write the amount of shading as:
a fraction ____________
a decimal ____________
a percent ____________

Name ______________________________ Date ____________

FDP Tug Of War

There are some things in life that you just must know. The FDP Tug of War Cards will help you learn the 15 most common fraction, decimal, and percent equivalences.

This exciting game can be played with between 2 and 4 players. Each group of students will need a deck of FDP Tug of War Cards (reproduced from pages 30–32).

To Play:

1. Shuffle all of the cards. Evenly distribute the cards among the players.
2. All players must keep their cards face down. (No peeking!)
3. The player to the left of the dealer turns over his or her top card. Proceeding clockwise, all other players then turn over their top cards.
4. The player who has turned over the FDP Card with the greatest value wins the round. He or she picks up all cards.
5. Play continues in this fashion until all of the cards have been played.
6. In the event that two equivalent cards are played at the same time, and these cards hold the highest value in that round, then a war occurs.
7. To determine the winner of the war, each player with an equivalent high card lays down a second card. The player whose card has the highest value wins all of the cards on the table.
8. The winner of the game is the player with the most cards.

Tug Of War Cards

Fraction	Decimal	Percent	Fraction	Decimal	Percent	Fraction	Decimal	Percent
		25%		0.125			0.8	

Fraction	Decimal	Percent	Fraction	Decimal	Percent	Fraction	Decimal	Percent
$\frac{1}{4}$			$\frac{12.5}{100}$			$\frac{80}{100}$		

Fraction	Decimal	Percent	Fraction	Decimal	Percent	Fraction	Decimal	Percent
$\frac{1}{8}$			$\frac{4}{5}$			$\frac{3}{8}$		

Fraction	Decimal	Percent	Fraction	Decimal	Percent	Fraction	Decimal	Percent
		12½%			80%			45%

Fraction	Decimal	Percent
83/100		

Fraction	Decimal	Percent
7/8		

Fraction	Decimal	Percent
		66⅔%

Fraction	Decimal	Percent
40/100		

Fraction	Decimal	Percent
		87½%

Fraction	Decimal	Percent
	0.6	

Fraction	Decimal	Percent
2/5		

Fraction	Decimal	Percent
	0.875	

Fraction	Decimal	Percent
66.6/100		

Fraction	Decimal	Percent
	0.4	

Fraction	Decimal	Percent
87.5/100		

Fraction	Decimal	Percent
		70%

Fraction	Decimal	Percent
		40%

Fraction	Decimal	Percent
75/100		

Fraction	Decimal	Percent
	0.7	

Fraction	Decimal	Percent
1/3		

Fraction	Decimal	Percent
	0.75	

Fraction	Decimal	Percent
70/100		

Fraction	Decimal	Percent
		33⅓%

Fraction	Decimal	Percent
		75%

Fraction	Decimal	Percent
7/10		

Fraction	Decimal	Percent
	0.33	

Fraction	Decimal	Percent
3/4		

Fraction	Decimal	Percent
25/100		

Fraction	Decimal	Percent
33.3/100		

Fraction	Decimal	Percent
2/3		

Fraction	Decimal	Percent
	0.25	

Fraction	Decimal	Percent
	0.625	

Fraction	Decimal	Percent
20/100		

Fraction	Decimal	Percent
	0.16	

Fraction	Decimal	Percent
		62½%

Fraction	Decimal	Percent
	0.2	

Fraction	Decimal	Percent
16/100		

Fraction	Decimal	Percent
5/8		

Fraction	Decimal	Percent
1/5		

Fraction	Decimal	Percent
3/5		

Fraction	Decimal	Percent
62.5/100		

Fraction	Decimal	Percent
50/100		

Fraction	Decimal	Percent
		60%

Fraction	Decimal	Percent
	0.3	

Fraction	Decimal	Percent
1/2		

Fraction	Decimal	Percent
	0.6	

Fraction	Decimal	Percent
30/100		

Fraction	Decimal	Percent
		50%

Fraction	Decimal	Percent
60/100		

Fraction	Decimal	Percent
3/10		

Fraction	Decimal	Percent
	0.5	

Fraction	Decimal	Percent
5/6		

Fraction	Decimal	Percent
		30%

Fraction	Decimal	Percent
1/6		

Fraction	Decimal	Percent
		83⅓%

Fraction	Decimal	Percent
		20%

Fraction	Decimal	Percent
		16⅔%

Fraction	Decimal	Percent
	0.83	

EXPONENT BINGO

Each member of the class has a 4-by-4 grid and writes one of the following numbers in each box in any order:

1, 2, 3, 4, 5, 6, 8, 9, 10, 16, 25, 27, 32, 36, 49, 64, 81, 100, 125, 216, 256

The host of the game reads the following exponent problems in random order. (The answer is included in the parentheses next to the problem.) The host should not read the answer to the class members.

Each player solves the exponent problem and circles the answer on the grid. The first student to circle four answers in a row, either vertically, horizontally, or diagonally, is the winner.

1. 6 to the zero power (1)
2. 5 to the first power (5)
3. 2 squared (4)
4. 2 cubed (8)
5. 4 squared (16)
6. 2 to the fifth power (32)
7. 6 squared (36)
8. 7 squared (49)
9. 3 cubed (27)
10. 3 to the first power (3)
11. 5 cubed (125)
12. 4 to the fourth power (256)
13. 10 to the first power (10)
14. 8 squared (64)
15. 6 cubed (216)
16. 10 squared (100)
17. 3 to the fourth power (81)
18. 5 squared (25)
19. 3 squared (9)
20. 6 to the first power (6)
21. 2 to the first power (2)

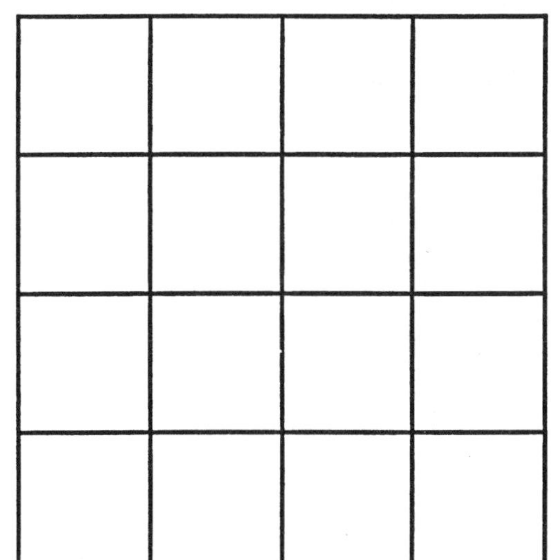

Name ______________________________ Date ____________

Part Two:

ALGEBRA READINESS

PROPERTY SHORTCUTS

Knowing the properties of addition is important as you begin studying algebra. Of course, knowing them is also extremely helpful to you any time you are working with numbers. Quickly review these properties:

The Commutative Property (Order Property)
You can add two addends (or numbers) in either order, and the sum will be the same.
Example: $4 + 3 = 3 + 4$

The Associative Property (Grouping Property)
You can group addends differently, and the sum will be the same.
Example: $1 + (7+3) = (1+7) + 3$

The Zero Property
When one of the addends is 0, the sum equals the other addend.
Example: $5 + 0 = 5$

Keep these important properties in mind. You may need to apply them in the following situations.

Situation #1

Mary Smart reviewed this worksheet and realized that she actually had to complete only four of the eight problems. Why does she think that? Is there a property that helped her arrive at this conclusion? Complete the problems below, and then describe how you think Mary completed this work.

Name Mary Smart

1. 475 + 525
2. 525 + 475
3. 1017 + 823
4. 823 + 1017
5. 1287 + 1488
6. 1488 + 1287
7. 1900 + 2090
8. 2090 + 1900

Explain Mary's response: ____________

____

____

____

Situation #2

Quick-working Quincy finished with the assignment below at least ten minutes before most of the other students. What was his strategy? Work the seven problems and then write how you think Quincy finished so quickly.

Name Q. W. Quincy

1. 73 + 27 + 482 = ____________
2. 57 + 89 + 11 = ____________
3. 9 + 11+ 62 = ____________
4. $6.00 + $ 4.00 + $14.00 = ______
5. $8.95 + $1.05 + $26.00 = ______
6. 175 + 25 + 47 = ____________
7. 99 + 1 + 234 = ____________

Write the secret to Quincy's speedy work:

____

____

____

Name ______________________ Date ____________

Algebra Readiness

ORDER, PLEASE!

In some cases, order is essential to ensure a correct response to an equation. In mathematics, when there is more than one operation to perform, a plan of action must be put into place.

First, remember to complete all operations inside the grouping symbols (parentheses) using the given order of operations. Second, rename any exponential expressions. Third, work all multiplication or division problems from left to right, whichever operation comes first. Fourth, work all addition or subtraction problems from left to right, whichever operation comes first.

Using the Hundred Number Board (page 37) as a game sheet, the students work in pairs to solve problems. Alternating turns, each student rolls five dice. Using the numbers displayed on the dice, the player has to write three mathematical expressions to claim three numbers on the board. Only expressions written correctly can capture a number square. Each correct expression earns the player ten points. If a player should land on a square adjacent to a captured square, then he or she wins an additional five points for each adjacent square.

Example:

Player 1 rolls a 2, 3, 5, 3, and 6.

The first expression written is as follows:

$(2 \times 3) + (5 \times 3) + 6 = 27$

The second expression written is as follows:

$(2 \times 3 \times 5) + (3 \times 6) = 48$

The third expression written is as follows:

$(2 \times 6 \times 3) - (5 + 3) = 28$

Scoring:

First expression .... 10 points
Second expression ... 10 points
Third expression...... 15 points
(10 points for the expression; 28 is adjacent to a previously captured square, so the player wins an additional 5 points)

(The second player may want to indicate his or her squares with a mark other than a circle, such as a square or an X, to distinguish them from those of Player 1.)

Hundred Number Board

1	2	3	4	5	6	7	8	9	10
11	12	13	14	15	16	17	18	19	20
21	22	23	24	25	26	27	28	29	30
31	32	33	34	35	36	37	38	39	40
41	42	43	44	45	46	47	48	49	50
51	52	53	54	55	56	57	58	59	60
61	62	63	64	65	66	67	68	69	70
71	72	73	74	75	76	77	78	79	80
81	82	83	84	85	86	87	88	89	90
91	92	93	94	95	96	97	98	99	100

Please Excuse My Dear Aunt Sally

This is a card game to increase the student's proficiency in working with order of operations. The following materials are needed: one die, scientific calculator, and game cards (the game card pattern is below). Make numerous copies of the game card pattern. Write as many expressions as you like on the game cards to create a full deck of cards (a deck of forty cards would allow four students to play ten rounds).

Making the game cards allows each teacher to address various mathematical levels. Possible expressions could include:

Please Excuse My Dear Aunt Sally	Please Excuse My Dear Aunt Sally
$4(3+2) \div 10$	$3(10 \div 5) + 4^2$
Please Excuse My Dear Aunt Sally	**Please Excuse My Dear Aunt Sally**
$5 + 2 \bullet 6 - 2$	$3^2 + 9 - (5 \bullet 2 - 6) \div 2$

Each player is given a card and must determine its value using order of operations. The player rolls a die to determine the point value that is to be added or deducted from his or her score. A score card can be used to keep score (pattern page 119). If the answer is correct, the player gains the number of points shown on the die. If the answer is incorrect, the player deducts the number of points shown on the die.

There should be a scorekeeper for the group who determines if a player has responded correctly by checking each response with the calculator. The role of the scorekeeper can be rotated among the members of the group. Play ends after ten rounds. Each player tallies his or her score and the scorekeeper checks everyone's scores. The player with the greatest number of points wins the game.

Please Excuse My Dear Aunt Sally	Please Excuse My Dear Aunt Sally
Please Excuse My Dear Aunt Sally	**Please Excuse My Dear Aunt Sally**

Are You More Like David Copperfield or Blaise Pascal?

David Copperfield is a well-known magician who has performed incredible feats of magic, such as making the Eiffel Tower disappear! His amazing act is based on tricking and fooling his observers. Blaise Pascal was a French mathematician and scientist who used an arithmetic triangle to solve problems.

You are going to solve some math problems. Will you use magic, like David Copperfield, or mathematics, like Pascal, to arrive at your solutions?

Look at each set of numbers below. In each set, four people have guessed a series of numbers and received a response telling whether their numbers fit the rule of the set. By looking at their guesses and the responses to their guesses, can you come up with the rule that applies to each set?

Set 1

Person	Guess	Response
	1, 2, 3	Yes
	10, 12, 14	No
	3, 5, 8	Yes
	12, 2, 14	Yes

The rule for Set 1 is the third number is the sum of the first and second numbers.

Using one of the correct responses in Set 1, write a number sentence to demonstrate the rule.

____

Set 2

Person	Guess	Response
	2, 3, 7	No
	6, 4, 2	Yes
	16, 8, 8	Yes
	70, 3, 67	Yes

The rule for Set 2 is ______________________

Using one of the correct responses in Set 2, write a number sentence to demonstrate the rule.

____

Name ______________________ Date ____________

Set 3

Person	Guess	Response
	28, 4, 7	Yes
	16, 8, 2	Yes
	7, 3, 9	No
	36, 12, 3	Yes

The rule for Set 3 is ______________________

____

Using one of the correct responses in Set 3, write a number sentence to demonstrate the rule.

____

Set 4

Person	Guess	Response
	2, 4, 7	Yes
	4, 3, 8	Yes
	1, 2, 4	Yes
	6, 3, 1	No

The rule for Set 4 is ______________________

____

Using one of the correct responses in Set 4, write a number sentence to demonstrate the rule.

____

Set 5

Person	Guess	Response
	8, 3, 4	Yes
	7, 2, 4	Yes
	8, 9, 3	No
	11, 4, 6	Yes

The rule for Set 5 is ______________________

____

Using one of the correct responses in Set 5, write a number sentence to demonstrate the rule.

____

Set 6

Person	Guess	Response
	2, 4, 8	Yes
	6, 8, 16	Yes
	4, 8, 12	No
	8, 10, 20	Yes

The rule for Set 6 is ______________________

____

Using one of the correct responses in Set 6, write a number sentence to demonstrate the rule.

____

Name ______________________________ Date ______________

The Land Of Unknown

Mary Variable and Connie Constant would like to invite each of you on a journey into the unknown. Mary Variable is your tour director. Connie Constant is her assistant and will substitute for her in different places. Before we begin our journey into the Land of Unknown in the year of Changing Times, there are a few questions you must answer.

In your own words, write a definition for the word **constant.**

____

____

Use the word **constant** in a sentence.

____

____

In your own words, write a definition for the word **vary.**

____

____

Use the word **vary** in a sentence.

____

____

Think about the word variable. It is a noun. Variable is not a place or a person, so it must be a thing. With the word vary (verb) in mind, write a definition for variable in your own words. (Think about your definition of vary before you begin writing.)

____

____

Name ________________________________ Date ____________

The Land Of Unknown

Mary Variable and Connie Constant are a unique pair of friends. Together their friendship seems to perform magic. Depending on the roll of the dice even their mood may change. Mary's last name gives a clue to her personality. "Variable" means something unknown and subject to change.

You will engage in a game that will show you how these two young ladies work so well together. Connie Constant is ready to be substituted for Mary Variable at any time. What a good standby!

This game is designed for two or four players. You will need one die, one alpha cube (labeled with a, a, b, b, c, c), a pencil, one sheet of paper, a deck of variable cards (page 43), and game board (page 44).

To Play:

1. Shuffle the variable cards, and then place them on the table, face up.
2. Player 1 rolls the die and the alpha cube.
3. The letter showing on the alpha cube determines the variable the player will insert into the equation (either choice a, b, or c).
4. Player 1 then answers the equation using his or her chosen variable.
5. If Player 1 solves the problem correctly, he or she moves forward on the game board the number of spaces indicated by the roll of the die. If the problem is solved incorrectly, the player loses a turn.
6. If the players use all of the cards in the deck, they can reshuffle the deck and start again.

Example:

Variable Card Reads
$5 + x =$ ________ if
a. x is –3
b. x is 17
c. x is –7

Player 1 rolls b, 6. He or she must substitute choice b (17) in the equation. If Player 1 answers "22" (the correct response to the equation 5 + 17) the player moves ahead 6 spaces on the game board. If the player answers incorrectly, he or she loses a turn.

VARIABLE CARDS

$5 + x =$ ___ if a. x is –3 b. x is 17 c. x is –7	$(x + 5) \div 2 =$ ___ if a. x is 11 b. x is 95 c. x is 0	$2^x =$ ___ if a. x is 3 b. x is 5 c. x is 0	$(-5)^x =$ ___ if a. x is 3 b. x is 2 c. x is 1
$(24 \div x) - 1 =$ ___ if a. x is 4 b. x is 12 c. x is –2	$x^3 =$ ___ if a. x is 3 b. x is 5 c. x is –1	$6x^2 =$ ___ if a. x is 3 b. x is 1 c. x is 0	$-5^x =$ ___ if a. x is 3 b. x is 2 c. x is 1
$2(x - 19) =$ ___ if a. x is 100 b. x is 37 c. x is –19	$40 \div x =$ ___ if a. x is 5 b. x is –20 c. x is 60	$x^2 + 4x + 4 =$ ___ if a. x is 3 b. x is 5 c. x is 0	$(-x)^4 =$ ___ if a. x is 2 b. x is 1 c. x is 0
$9x =$ ___ if a. x is 4 b. x is 13 c. x is –6	$(x + 7) \div 3 =$ ___ if a. x is 5 b. x is 53 c. x is 0	$(x + 1)^2 =$ ___ if a. x is 6 b. x is 4 c. x is 1	$(-4)^x =$ ___ if a. x is 3 b. x is 2 c. x is 1
$x + 7 =$ ___ if a. x is 8 b. x is 93 c. x is –14	$x^4 =$ ___ if a. x is 2 b. x is 3 c. x is –1	$(3x)^2 =$ ___ if a. x is 1 b. x is 2 c. x is 0	$-4^x =$ ___ if a. x is 3 b. x is 2 c. x is 1
$(72 \div x) + 5 =$ ___ if a. x is 6 b. x is 9 c. x is –8	$3^x =$ ___ if a. x is 2 b. x is 4 c. x is 1	$56 - 6x =$ ___ if a. x is 8 b. x is 1 c. x is 0	$-x =$ ___ if a. x is 5 b. x is –3 c. x is –1
$4(x - 31) =$ ___ if a. x is 80 b. x is 57 c. x is 10	$4x^2 =$ ___ if a. x is 3 b. x is 0 c. x is 5	$(x + 2)^2 =$ ___ if a. x is 3 b. x is 5 c. x is 0	$(-1)(x) =$ ___ if a. x is 5 b. x is –3 c. x is –1
$7x =$ ___ if a. x is 8 b. x is 11 c. x is –6	$x^2 + 2x + 1 =$ ___ if a. x is 6 b. x is 4 c. x is 1	$(5x)^2 =$ ___ if a. x is 1 b. x is 2 c. x is 0	$15 \div x =$ ___ if a. x is 5 b. x is –3 c. x is –1
$30 \div x =$ ___ if a. x is 6 b. x is –90 c. x is 45	$(-x)^2 =$ ___ if a. x is 3 b. x is 1 c. x is –2	$108 - 8x =$ ___ if a. x is 12 b. x is 1 c. x is 0	$x + 3 =$ ___ if a. x is –5 b. x is 3 c. x is 0

The Land of Unknown Game Board

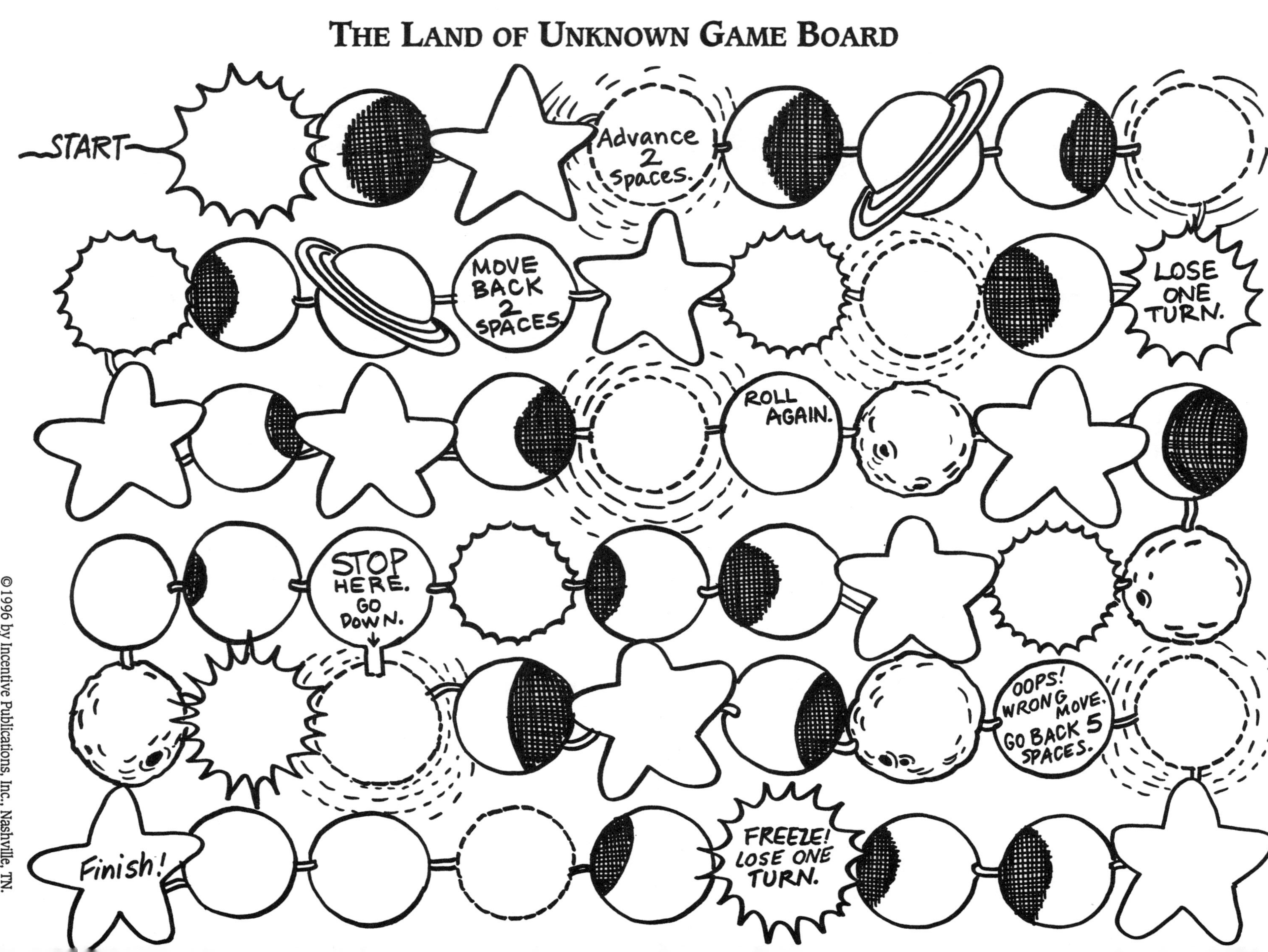

KEEP ON TRACKING

To the teacher:

Write each of the following expressions on the footprint patterns (page 46) for students to solve. (Include the numbers 1–25 on the patterns.)

1. $2x - 3y + 6x$
2. $9a + 3a + 6$
3. $3y + 2y - 4y$
4. $x + 2y - x - 3y$
5. $9b + 8b - c$
6. $4y - 3x + 10y + 2x$
7. $6a - 7 - 5a + 7$
8. $3x - 2y + 4x + 5y$
9. $6a - 2 - 5a + 3 + 5a$
10. $-6x - 5 - 3x + 2 - 7x$
11. $2b - 2b + 4 - 7$
12. $4x + 2 + 4x - 5$
13. $7b^2 + 9b - 4b^2$
14. $3x^2 + 2x + 5x^2$
15. $-5 + 6 + 2a + 3a$
16. $-3ab + 2a + 6ab$
17. $11xy + 12y + 9xy$
18. $5x^2y + 3xy^2 + 4x^2y$
19. $4ab + 6ab - 5 + 2$
20. $-7x - 2x - 9 + 10$
21. $10x^2 + 5 - 5x^2 + 6$
22. $-4b - 3 + 8b + 7$
23. $5y^2 + 9y - 3y^2 - 6y$
24. $4x^2 + 3x + 2 - 3x + 2$
25. $3a + 6b - 4a + 2$

Then, give them the following directions:

Inspector Poly observed strange footprints leading into the jungle and wondered who was lost in the wild. He found a message left behind that stated, "To discover who I am, you must track down my like terms." The Inspector discovered more footprints than he was able to identify, and now he requests your assistance. The Inspector has provided you with this clue: You must combine like terms to identify each footprint. Like terms are those terms with the same variables to the same power. After combining each expression's like terms, find the corresponding expression in the solution set. Write that letter next to each answer in the matching blank below (numbers correspond with numbers 1 through 25 above) to find out who was lost in the jungle.

Solution Set

(A) $4x^2 + 4$	(M) $8x - 3$	(C) $20xy + 12y$	(E) $8x - 3y$	(L) a
(E) $3ab + 2a$	(N) $6a + 1$	(E) $3b^2 + 9b$	(I) $14y - x$	(O) $-a + 6b + 2$
(T) $7x + 3y$	(D) $12a + 6$	(K) $-16x - 3$	(M) y	(S) $5a + 1$
(Y) $5x^2 + 11$	(H) $10ab - 3$	(T) $17b - c$	(V) $9x^2y + 3x^2$	(T) $8x^2 + 2x$
(C) $-9x + 1$	(E) -3	(M) $-y$	(A) $2y^2 + 3y$	(I) $4b + 4$

___ ___ ___ ___ ___ ___ ___ ___ ___   ___ ___ ___ ___ ___ ___ ___ ___   ___ ___   ___ ___   ___ ___ ___ ___

2 3 8 16 20 5 22 18 11   4 24 14 19 7 25 17 10   6 15   3 21   9 23 12 1

Algebra Readiness

KEEP ON TRACKING PATTERNS

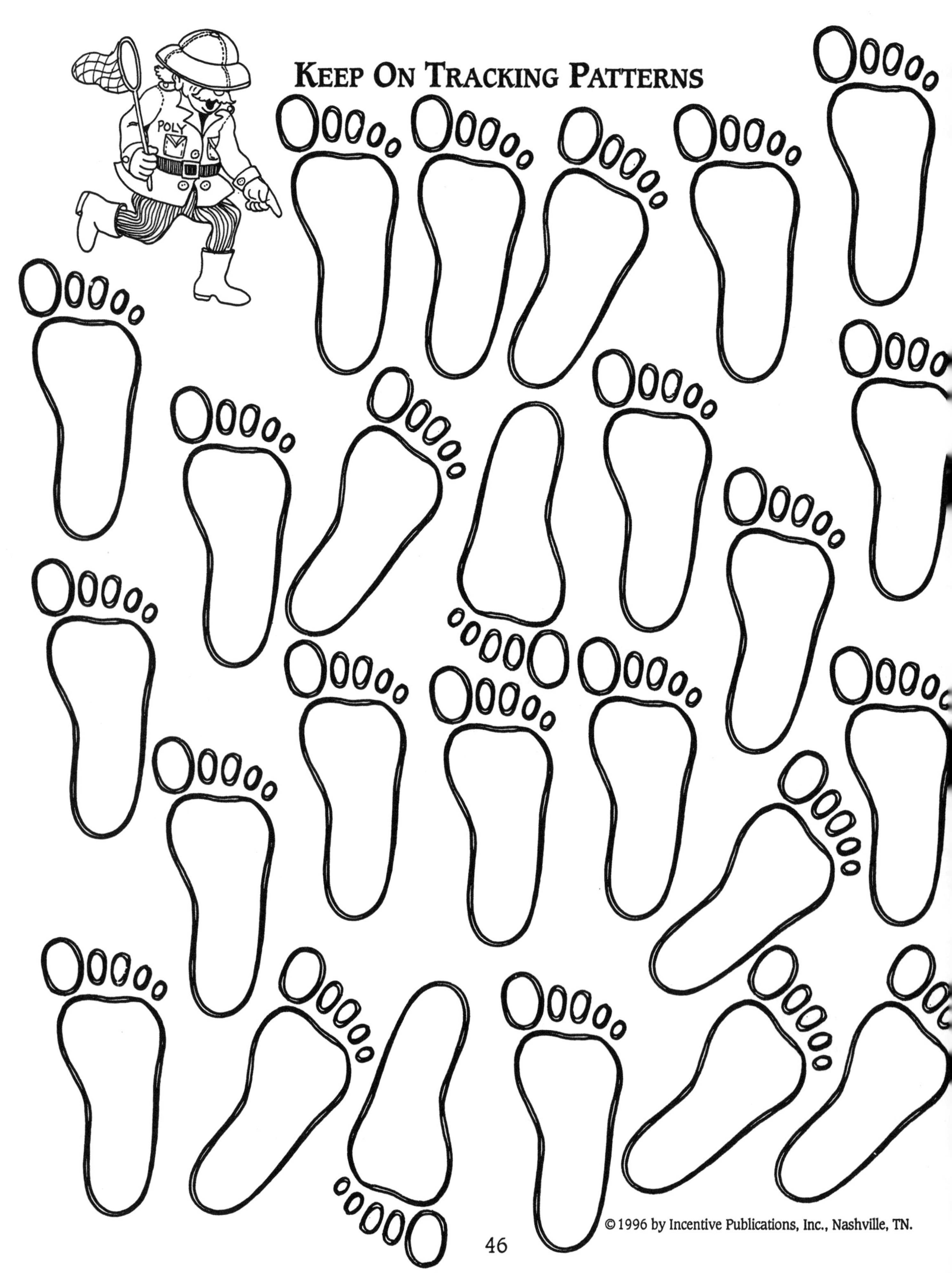

Can't Wait To Evaluate!

To Play:

1. Separate the class into cooperative groups of four members each. Give each group a deck of cards (patterns, pages 47–49) and a die.
2. The dealer gives each player a card and rolls the die. Each player uses the number value on the die to evaluate his or her expression. Each player must explain to the group the method used to determine the value of the expression. The player with the highest value wins all of the cards in that round (this constitutes a book). The player at the end of the game with the most books is the winner.

GAME VARIATION: The game is played using two dice of different colors, one representing a positive number and the other a negative number. The dealer rolls the dice to determine the integer value to be substituted in each expression. Follow the same rules as above. The role of the dealer should be rotated.

Evaluation Cards

Can't Wait To Evaluate	Can't Wait To Evaluate	Can't Wait To Evaluate
$-3x^2 - x^0$	$x(2x + 2)$	$5x^2 + 6x - 6$
Can't Wait To Evaluate	**Can't Wait To Evaluate**	**Can't Wait To Evaluate**
$x(x - 1)$	$\frac{x}{x^0}$	$x^3 - 3$
Can't Wait To Evaluate	**Can't Wait To Evaluate**	**Can't Wait To Evaluate**
$\frac{x + x + x}{x}$	$-2x - 5$	$-5x^2 - 3x + 10$
Can't Wait To Evaluate	**Can't Wait To Evaluate**	**Can't Wait To Evaluate**
$\frac{x}{x}$	$\frac{x^2}{x}$	$x^2 - 4$

Algebra Readiness

Can't Wait To Evaluate	Can't Wait To Evaluate	Can't Wait To Evaluate
$3x + 2(x + 3)$	$4x + 3(-x + 2)$	$x + x^2$
Can't Wait To Evaluate $\frac{x^2 - 1}{x + 1}$	**Can't Wait To Evaluate** $2x + 5$	**Can't Wait To Evaluate** $-x + x^2$

Can't Wait To Evaluate	Can't Wait To Evaluate	Can't Wait To Evaluate
$3x + 4$	$-(x)^2$	$x + x^2 + x^3$
Can't Wait To Evaluate $(-x)^2$	**Can't Wait To Evaluate** $-x$	**Can't Wait To Evaluate** $\frac{x^2 + 12x + 20}{x + 2}$

Can't Wait To Evaluate	Can't Wait To Evaluate	Can't Wait To Evaluate
$2x - 4$	x^3	$x^0 + x^1 + x^2$
Can't Wait To Evaluate $(x)^0$	**Can't Wait To Evaluate** x^2	**Can't Wait To Evaluate** $3x - 4$

Can't Wait To Evaluate $3x + 4x - 3x$	Can't Wait To Evaluate $6x^2 - 8x - 8$	Can't Wait To Evaluate $-3x - 4$
Can't Wait To Evaluate $10x^2 + x - 9$	Can't Wait To Evaluate $-x(8 - 2x)$	Can't Wait To Evaluate $x^2 + 4x + 4$

Can't Wait To Evaluate $x^2 - 25$	Can't Wait To Evaluate $-4x + 3x - 1$	Can't Wait To Evaluate $-3x + 4$
Can't Wait To Evaluate $\frac{4x + 12}{-4}$	Can't Wait To Evaluate $4x + 9$	Can't Wait To Evaluate $\frac{x^2 + 6x + 9}{x + 3}$

Can't Wait To Evaluate $x^2 - x - 6$	Can't Wait To Evaluate x

POLLY WANTS A MATCHING PAIR!

Arrange the students in cooperative groups of four members each. Each group receives a deck of cards (pages 51–53). Each player is dealt seven cards. The top card of the remaining deck is turned face up, placed next to the deck. This becomes the discard pile. Players take turns drawing a card from the deck or taking the top card in the discard pile. In each round, the player must lay down matching pairs and then discard one card. The game ends when a player runs out of cards. The winner is the first person to discard all of his or her cards. Each player receives ten points for each pair. The winner gets one additional point for each card remaining in each opponent's hand.

An Example Of A Winning Hand:

The player finishes the game with three matching pairs. The matching pairs may be the following:

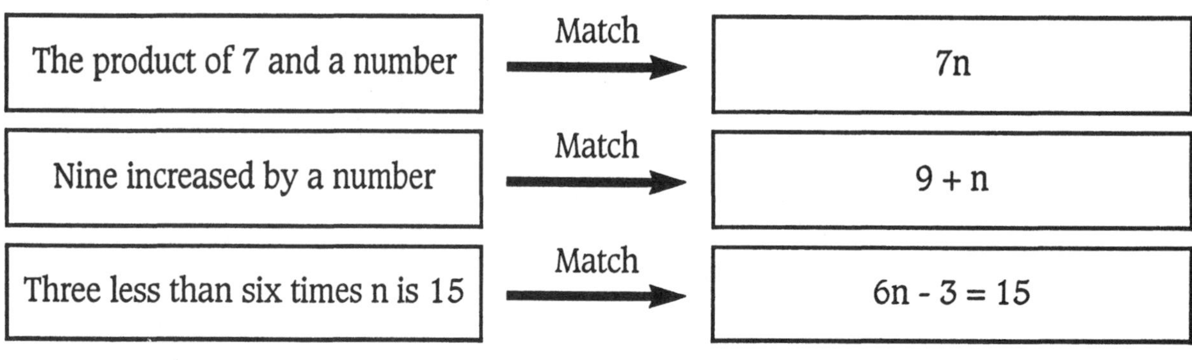

An Example Of An Opponent's Hand:

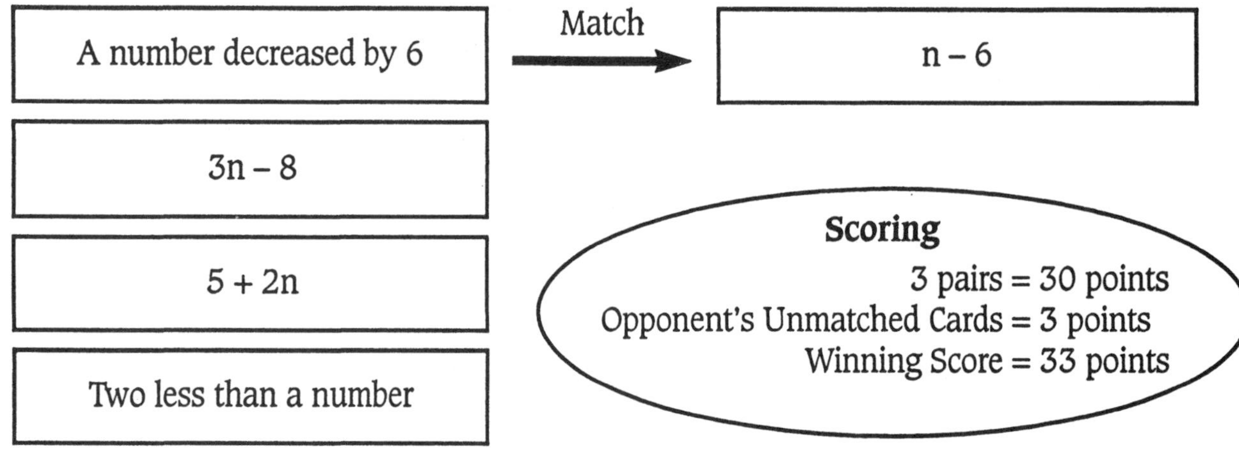

MATCHING PAIR CARDS

Seven times a number is the same as 10 more than twice the number	Nine less than 5 times a number is the same as the number decreased by 1	Seven less than a number is twice the number	Four times the sum of a number and 10 is 8
Five times the sum of 6 and x is the same as 2 increased by x	Ten less than 8 times the sum of twice a number and –4	Fourteen more than a number is 3 times the number	Seven more than 6 times the sum of a number and 4
Ten more than a number is 3 times the sum of the number and 4	Seven less than twice a number is the same as the number decreased by 8	Five increased by 3 less than twice a number	A number increased by 20 is 8 decreased by 3 times the number
Five times the sum of 7 and x is the same as 11 increased by x	A number increased by 16 is the same as 4 decreased by 3 times the number	Five times a number is the same as 6 more than twice the number	Four more than 5 times a number is the same as 3 times the number
Four more than a number is the same as 3 times the sum of the number and 2	Nine more than 8 times a number is the same as 7 times the number	The product of 7 and a number	The sum of a number and 3
A number decreased by 9	Ten more than twice a number	Nine increased by a number	A number decreased by 6
Five times the sum of x and 7	Four increased by a number is 20	Five more than twice a number	Two less than a number
Three times the sum of x and 4 is 21	Eight more than twice a number is 14	Eight less than 3 times a number	One more than the sum of x and 6
Seven increased by a number	Four less than a number	Six times the sum of 3 and a number	Seven less than twice the sum of a number and 5

Nine less than 4 times a number	A number decreased by 7	Six decreased by 3 times a number equals –9	Seven more than 4 times a number is 15
Seven times a number is 35	Three less than 6 times a number is 15	Four less than 6 times a number is 44	Eight increased by the sum of a number and 5 is 3
Eight more than 3 times a number is 2	Twelve increased by 4 times a number is 2	The product of 6 and a number	The sum of a number and 8
Five less than 6 times a number is 7	Nine decreased by twice a number is 1	A number increased by 5 times the number is –30	Eight decreased by 5 times a number is 18
Three times the sum of a number and –2 is 15	Twelve decreased by 5 times the sum of a number and 7	$7x$	$x + 3$
$x + 4 = 3(x + 2)$	$9 + 8x = 7x$	$9 + x$	$x - 6$
$x - 9$	$10 + 2x$	$5 + 2x$	$x - 2$
$5(x + 7)$	$4 + x = 20$	$3x - 8$	$(x + 6) + 1$
$3(x + 4) = 21$	$8 + 2x = 14$	$7x = 10 + 2x$	$5x - 9 = x - 1$

$x - 7 = 2x$	$4(x + 10) = 8$	$5(x + 6) = 2 + x$	$8[2x + (-4)] - 10$
$14 + x = 3x$	$6(x + 4) + 7$	$x + 10 = 3(x + 4)$	$2x - 7 = x - 8$
$5 + (2x - 3)$	$x + 20 = 8 - 3x$	$5(7 + x) = 11 + x$	$x + 16 = 4 - 3x$
$5x = 6 + 2x$	$4 + 5x = 3x$	$6(3 + x)$	$2(x + 5) - 7$
$7 + x$	$x - 4$	$6 - 3x = -9$	$7 + 4x = 15$
$4x - 9$	$x - 7$	$6x - 4 = 44$	$8 + (x + 5) = 3$
$7x = 35$	$6x - 3 = 15$	$6x$	$x + 8$
$3x + 8 = 2$	$12 + 4x = 20$	$6x - 5 = 7$	$9 - 2x = 1$
$x + 5x = -30$	$8 - 5x = 18$	$3[x + (-2)] = 15$	$12 - 5(x + 7)$

PROPERTY FOR SALE

Sometime in the 21st century, properties became a hot commodity. Mathland Real Estate Company decided to auction certain properties away, but there was one catch. To take part in this auction, the participants had to be knowledgeable about certain kinds of properties, including:

- Commutative Property of Addition and Multiplication
- Associative Property of Addition and Multiplication
- Distributive Property
- Inverse Property of Addition and Multiplication
- Identity Element of Multiplication
- Multiplication Property of –1
- Multiplication Property of Zero
- Identity Element of Addition
- Substitution Property
- Transitive Property
- Symmetric Property
- Reflexive Property
- Closure Property of Addition and Multiplication

The auction participants soon found out that "knowledge is power" because the more they knew, the less it cost them. Their knowledge of the different properties allowed each participant to gain additional assets.

Two real estate companies participated in the auction. Equality Adjusters and Inequality Adjusters decided to compete to see who could acquire the most property. Each company hoped that they would walk away with the greatest holdings.

To Play:

Divide the class into two teams: Equality Adjusters and Inequality Adjusters. Every member of each company must participate in the auction or the company will default and their loans will be called in.

To Begin The Auction:

The auctioneer selects a property to go up for bid. Alternating turns, members of each company will bid on a property by stating the name of the mathematical property. If answered correctly, the property becomes an asset to that particular company, and the company acquires the real estate value listed on the property card. If answered incorrectly, the property value becomes a debt. The other company then has the option to name the property. If named correctly, the challenger acquires the property and the property value is doubled. If named incorrectly, the challenger must pay a penalty of $1000.

Play continues in this fashion until all property has been auctioned. The company with the highest property value wins.

Algebra Readiness

Property Cards

A	B	C	D
Property For Sale Value: $1000 $4 + (a + b) = (a + b) + 4$	Property For Sale Value: $2000 $14 + 16 = 16 + 14$	Property For Sale Value: $3000 (math) x $^1/_{(math)}$ = 1	Property For Sale Value: $4000 There is only one real number that is the sum of 2.1 and 0.5.
E Property For Sale Value: $1000 $xy = yx$	**F** Property For Sale Value: $2000 $(a) + (b) + (-a) = (b)$	**G** Property For Sale Value: $3000 There is only one real number that is the product of 5 and 6.	**H** Property For Sale Value: $4000 Can zero be a multiplication identity element? Why or why not?
I Property For Sale Value: $1000 $(4 + y) + z = 4 + (y + z)$	**J** Property For Sale Value: $2000 $1(a + b) = a + b$	**K** Property For Sale Value: $3000 $ab + cd + (-ab) = cd$	**L** Property For Sale Value: $4000 Can one be an addition identity element? Why or why not?
M Property For Sale Value: $1000 $-41 + 0 = -41$	**N** Property For Sale Value: $2000 Zero plus seven equals seven.	**O** Property For Sale Value: $3000 $(6a)(8x)(^1/_6 a) = 8x$	**P** Property For Sale Value: $4000 Can a property ever be false? Why or why not?
Q Property For Sale Value: $1000 $1(b) = b$	**R** Property For Sale Value: $2000 $(5 + q) + (-3) = (q + 5) + (-3)$	**S** Property For Sale Value: $3000 If "add" equals "increase" and "increase" equals "plus," then "add" equals "plus."	**T** Property For Sale Value: $4000 Use the Inverse Property of Addition to write an equivalent expression: (15) + (–15) = _____.

PROPERTY CARDS

U	V	W	X
Property For Sale Value: $1000 (12)(–8) = (–8)(12)	Property For Sale Value: $2000 3 x (9 x 0) = (3 x 9) x 0	Property For Sale Value: $3000 If w + 2 = 7 and 7 = 5 + 2, then w + 2 = 5 + 2.	Property For Sale Value: $4000 Use the Commutative Property of Addition to write an equivalent expression: (5) + (–5) = __.
Y	**Z**	**AA**	**BB**
Property For Sale Value: $1000 (4m)n = 4(mn)	Property For Sale Value: $2000 (a + b) + c = a + (b + c)	Property For Sale Value: $3000 If 6 = 3 + 3, then 3 + 3 = 6	Property For Sale Value: $4000 Use the Multiplication Property of One to write an equivalent expression: (5x)(1) = __.
CC	**DD**	**EE**	**FF**
Property For Sale Value: $1000 (0.5)(0) = 0	Property For Sale Value: $2000 –1(–3x – 5) = 3x + 5	Property For Sale Value: $3000 9 + 5 = (6 + 3) + 5	Property For Sale Value: $4000 Use the Distributive Property to write an equivalent expression: –4(x + 2) = __.
GG	**HH**	**II**	**JJ**
Property For Sale Value: $1000 5a + 2b = 2b + 5a	Property For Sale Value: $2000 (SU)M = S(UM)	Property For Sale Value: $3000 Every real number is equal to itself.	Property For Sale Value: $4000 Use the Associative Property of Addition to write an equivalent expression: (b + 4) + 5 = __.
KK	**LL**	**MM**	**NN**
Property For Sale Value: $1000 –1(a) = –a	Property For Sale Value: $2000 2(5a) + 2(4a) = 2(5a + 4a)	Property For Sale Value: $3000 3 + (2 + 1) = 3 + 3	Property For Sale Value: $4000 **n** times the quantity **a** plus **b** equals **n** times **a** plus **n** times **b**.

Opposites Attract

An ordinary deck of cards can assist you in understanding integers. The object of the game is to be the first player to discard all the cards from your hand. In the deck, the black cards will represent positive integers, and the red cards will represent negative integers.

To Play:

1. After removing all of the face cards except the Ace, the dealer shuffles the cards and deals five cards to each player. The Ace represents the value of 1.
2. The remaining cards in the deck are placed face down (draw pile) on the table. The dealer turns the top card over and places it face up next to the deck. This will become the discard pile.
3. The player to the dealer's left begins the game. He or she draws a card from either the discard pile or draw pile.
4. If the player has two or more cards that form a set of opposites (no more than three cards), he or she places them face up on the table as a set. The player must give an explanation of the reason the cards are considered opposites. An example of a set could be a red 5 and a black 5. Another set could include three cards: a red 9 and a black 7 with a black 2.
5. One card must be placed in the discard pile by each player as his or her turn ends. However, a player who is playing the final cards in his or her hand does not have to discard to win the game.
6. Play continues until one person no longer has any cards in his or her hand. If there is no winner and there are no more cards in the draw pile, the discard pile is reshuffled and used as the draw pile.
7. A player is allowed to pick up as many cards as necessary from the discard pile to reach a desired card. However, all cards picked up must remain in the player's hand.
8. At the end of a round, the winner receives five points for each book of opposites displayed. The winner also receives an additional one point for each card left in each of the other player's hand. The other players also receive five points for each book of opposites they have displayed.
9. After ten rounds, the person with the highest score is the winner.

   Extension: When the students become proficient with this version, alter the game by including the face cards.
   Jacks = 11, Queens = 12, and Kings = 13.

Algebra Readiness

WHAT A HAND!

Do you need a hand teaching integers? Make enough hands with integer fingers for the entire class to each have one (pattern, page 59).

Give each student a hand pattern to determine its value. For example, the hand in Example One on page 59 has the following integer values: –9, 8, 7, 6, and –5. The sum (value) of this hand is 7. Each student records his or her answer and then checks the results with another student. Once the students have arrived at their answers, you can extend the activity with the following ideas:

- Go around the room consecutively, asking each student to compare the value of his or her hand with that of a neighbor. Ask the student, "Is your hand greater than, less than, or equal to the student in front of you?"
- Have the students arrange themselves from least to greatest (or greatest to least), according to the sum of the integers on the hands. This can be done by rows or by forming a total class number line.
- Have the students find the grand total of all of the integer hands. Permit the students to determine a strategy to accomplish this. (A calculator might come in "handy"!)
- After the introduction of this operation, the hands can be used to provide students with practice in the other skills, including subtraction, multiplication, and division.
- "Give Me What?" is another way to use the hand patterns. On each hand, label only four fingers with integers (see Example Two, page 59). Distribute the hands among the class. Each student finds the sum of the four fingers and checks the answer with another student. Then call out a random value. Each student uses his or her sum to calculate the value of the missing finger so that it matches the value you called out. For example, you say, "Give me –13." If a student's hand has 3, –3, 5 and –9, she would say "–9."

Algebra Readiness

What A Hand!

Greatest, Least, and Absolute

Deal all of the cards from a deck of playing cards to the players. (Two to six players may play with one deck.) All players must have the same number of cards in their hands. If there are any extra cards, set them aside.

To Play:

This game is played in rounds. Altogether there will be nine rounds. In the first three rounds, the players are trying to play two cards that have the greatest combined value. The black cards represent positive integers. As a memory device, this can be linked to the phrase "in the black," meaning on the positive side of zero. The red cards represent negative integers. This can be linked to the phrase "in the red," meaning on the negative side of zero. The face cards have numerical value. The Jack is worth 11 points, the Queen is worth 12 points, and the King is worth 13 points. The Ace is worth 1 point.

Taking turns, each player lays down two cards and calls out the cards' combined value. For example, if the first player discards a black 10 and a red 2, he or she calls out, "Positive eight." The other players then must lay down two cards that are higher in value than 8. When all players have played two cards and called out the value of their combined cards, the player with the greatest value in that hand receives all the cards of the hand. Play continues until all cards are played.

To tally the score, all players count the cards they captured. Remember, the black cards are positive, and the red cards are negative. The player with the most points receives five points, the player with the second highest hand receives three points, and all other players receive one point each.

For the next three rounds, the players are required to play the cards that have the least combined value. Points are awarded after all cards are played. The player with the cards of the least value receives five points, the player with the second lowest hand receives three points, and all other players receive one point each.

For the final three rounds, the players are required to play hands that have the greatest absolute value. (This means that all cards regardless of color count as the value on the card.) Points are again awarded. The player whose cards have the greatest absolute value gets five points, the player with the second highest hand receives three points, and all other players receive one point each.

Additional Information:

- If an odd number of cards is given out to each player, the players will need to play three cards in the final hand.
- When teaching this game to the students, play only the first round (in which the students are playing for the greatest value). After they become proficient at this form of the game, introduce them to the other rounds (of least value and absolute value). A score card with all rounds is included on page 61.
- If you are playing this game with younger children, remove the face cards from the deck.

Greatest, Least, and Absolute Tally Sheet

	Rounds	Player 1	Player 2	Player 3	Player 4	Player 5	Player 6
Greatest Value	1						
	2						
	3						
Least Value	4						
	5						
	6						
Absolute Value	7						
	8						
	9						
	Total						

ABC Terrific!

An Integer Alphabet Card is a terrific way to reinforce the addition of integers. The Integer Alphabet can also be used in other disciplines to demonstrate how to apply mathematics to real life. What a great way to make an interdisciplinary connection!

Alphabet Integer Card

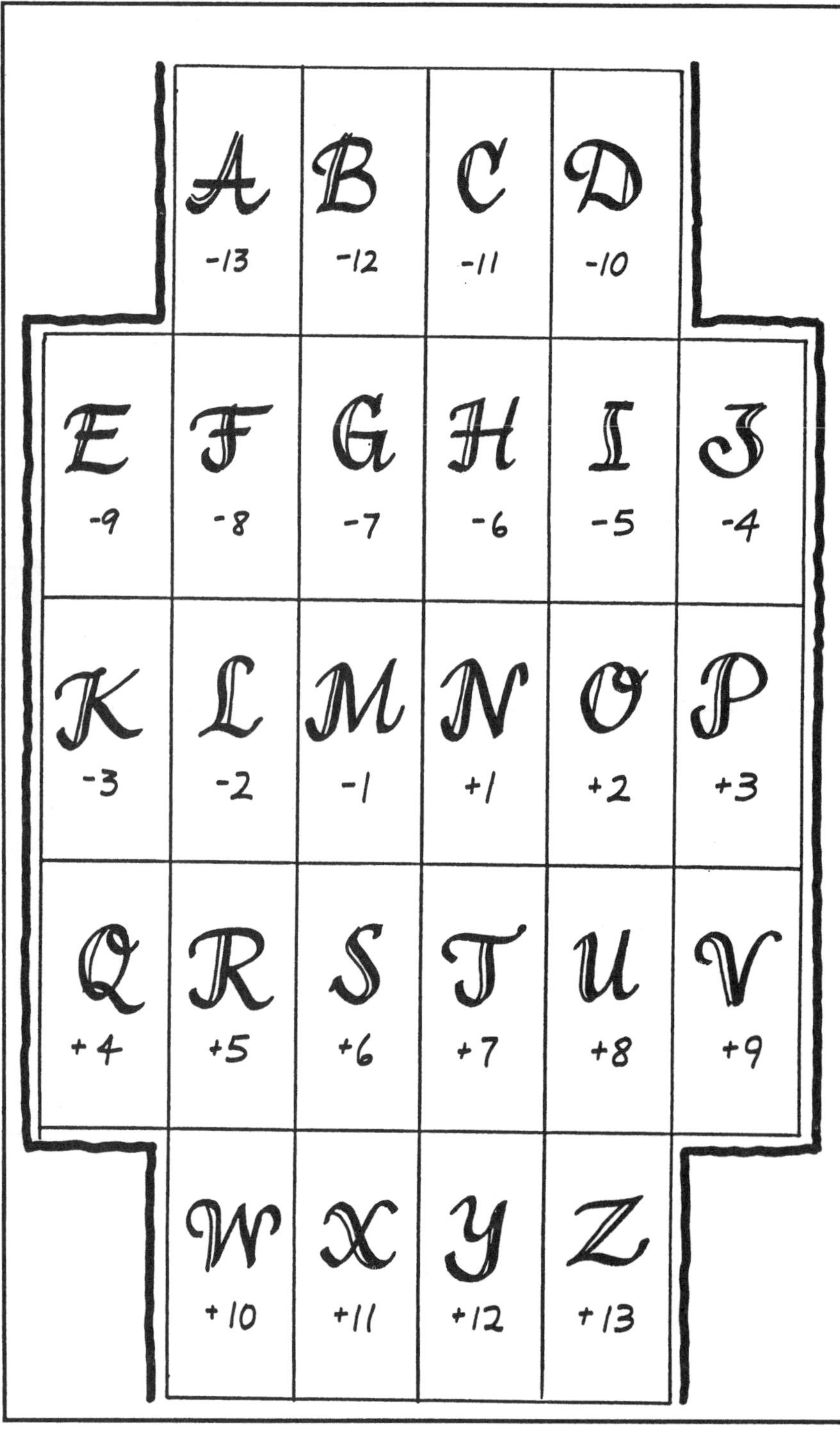

This activity can be used to reinforce other skills, such as comparing and ordering integers.

Students use the Integer Alphabet Card to find the value for each letter in a given word and then find the value of the word by determining the sum of the integer values.

A set of activity cards is included on page 63.

Example: "Math"

M	A	T	H
−1	−13	7	−6

−1 + −13 + 7 + −6
= −13
= Total Value of the Word

Integer Alphabet Activity Cards

Find the value of your first name and compare it to a classmate's. Is your name greater than, less than, or equal to your classmate's name?	Find the value of your last name and compare it to a classmate's. Is your last name greater than, less than, or equal to your classmate's name?	Have the class arrange themselves into a number line, from least to greatest, according to the value of their first name.
Try to find a five–letter word with the least possible value. Share your word with the class.	Try to find a five–letter word with the greatest possible value. Share your word with the class.	Find the value of the month in which you were born. Is it a "positive" month or "negative" month of the year?
Find the value of your favorite color name. Create a class bar graph of the integer values of everyone's favorite color. Identify the mean, median, and mode of the data.	Find the value of the name of your favorite pet. Out of everyone in the class, which pet's name has the greatest value and which has the least value?	Find the integer value of each of your spelling words.
Find a Halloween term that has the greatest integer value and the least integer value.	Make a list of ten words related to Thanksgiving and arrange them in order from least value to greatest value.	Add the value of your first name to the value of the first name of your boy– or girlfriend. If the value is positive, you have found true love!
Make a list of ten words related to St. Patrick's Day and find the integer value of each word. Give a partner the integer value and see if he or she can determine the word.	Find the value of the name of your ideal Christmas gift. If the value is positive, you just might find that gift under the tree this year. If the value is negative, better luck next year.	Find the integer value of both Abraham Lincoln and George Washington. Who was the "greater" president?
Separate the class into small groups and give each group several United States names. Have each group find the integer value of each state. Arrange all of the states in order from least value to greatest value.	Find the integer value for each of the following words: addition, subtraction, multiplication, and division. What relationship do these words have with each other?	Find the integer value of each of the following words: proper, improper, mixed, and whole. These words describe what kind of number?
Find the integer value of each of the following properties and give an example of each: commutative, associative, and distributive.	Unscramble the words below and then find each word's integer value: elapn, aqlue, usimn, scirenae, inpto, rgitene	Using a map, find a great place to take a summer vacation. Find the integer value of the country and the continent.

INTEGER ARITHMETIC

How can you encourage students to learn the rules of integers? The answer is letting them play cards. Cards can be used individually by students as flash cards, or they can be used to play a card game in a small cooperative group. These games serve as wonderful fillers for those unexpected free moments during the school day. Students often voluntarily choose to play a card game without being prompted by the teacher because students believe that they are playing a game. You realize, however, that they are practicing important skills.

Four card games, one for each integer operation, are found on pages 65–76. Students can play the addition game (pages 65–67) until they have internalized the rules of adding integers. Then, you can encourage the subtraction game (pages 68–70). The multiplication game (pages 71–73) and the division game (pages 74–76) can be added as you see fit. Six blank cards have been included in each group so that you may write in your own integer values.

To Play:

1. Assemble the students into groups of 2 or 4 players each.
2. Shuffle the cards and evenly distribute them among the players. Remember, just use one operation set at a time.
3. All players must keep their cards face down.
4. The player to the left of the dealer turns over his or her top card. Proceeding clockwise, all other players turn over their top cards.
5. The player who has turned over the integer card with the greatest value wins the set of cards. The winner picks up all of the cards in that hand. This will serve as a book. Each book is worth one point.
6. Play continues in this fashion until all cards have been played.
7. The winner of the game is the player with the most books.

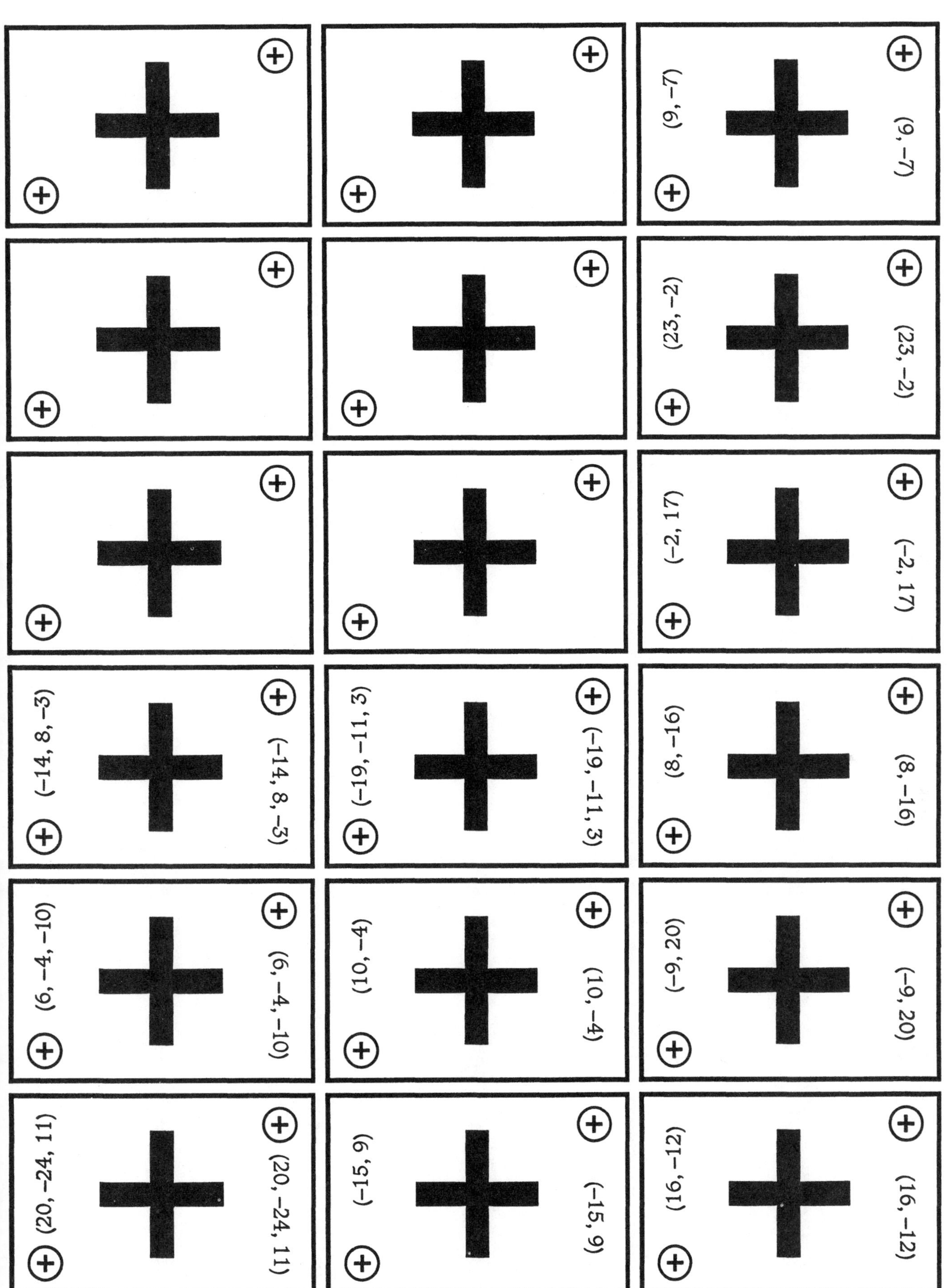
(9, −7)
(23, −2)
(−2, 17)
(−14, 8, −3)
(−19, −11, 3)
(8, −16)
(6, −4, −10)
(10, −4)
(−9, 20)
(20, −24, 11)
(−15, 9)
(16, −12)

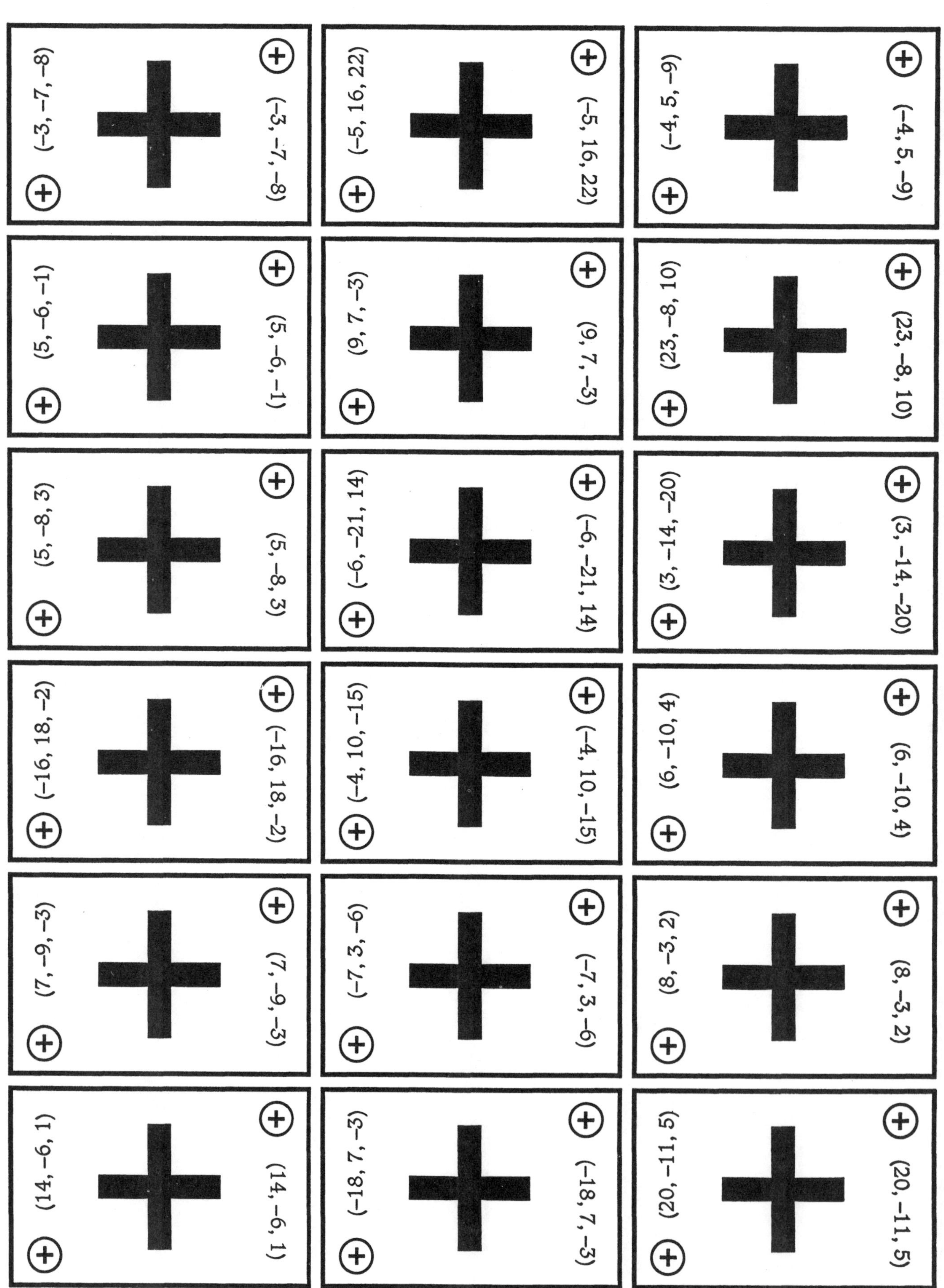
(-3, -7, -8)
(-3, -7, -8)
(-5, 16, 22)
(-5, 16, 22)
(-4, 5, -9)
(-4, 5, -9)
(5, -6, -1)
(5, -6, -1)
(9, 7, -3)
(9, 7, -3)
(23, -8, 10)
(23, -8, 10)
(5, -8, 3)
(5, -8, 3)
(-6, -21, 14)
(-6, -21, 14)
(3, -14, -20)
(3, -14, -20)
(-16, 18, -2)
(-16, 18, -2)
(-4, 10, -15)
(-4, 10, -15)
(6, -10, 4)
(6, -10, 4)
(7, -9, -3)
(7, -9, -3)
(-7, 3, -6)
(-7, 3, -6)
(8, -3, 2)
(8, -3, 2)
(14, -6, 1)
(14, -6, 1)
(-18, 7, -3)
(-18, 7, -3)
(20, -11, 5)
(20, -11, 5)

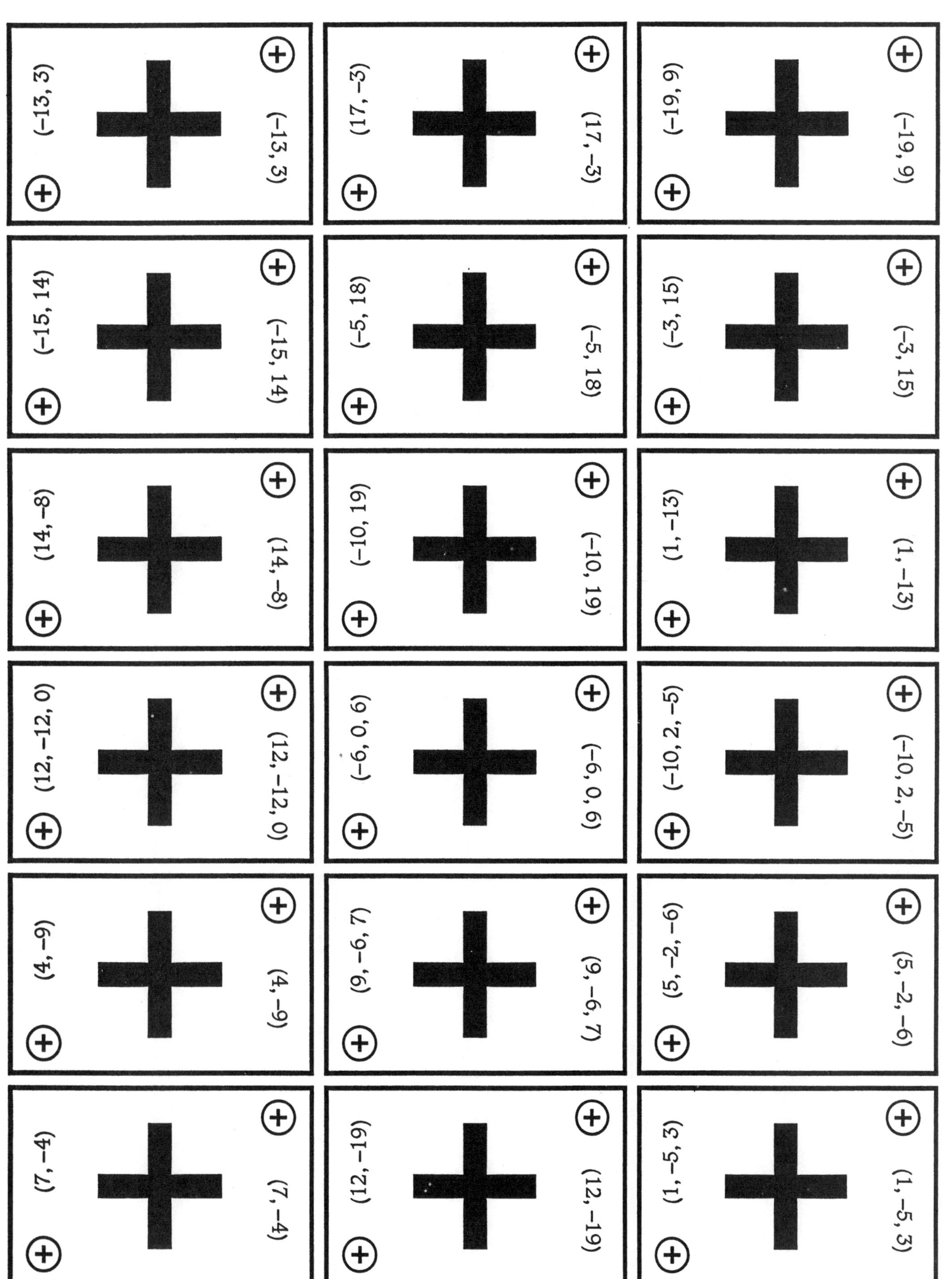

(−13, 3)
(17, −3)
(−19, 9)
(−15, 14)
(−5, 18)
(−3, 15)
(14, −8)
(−10, 19)
(1, −13)
(12, −12, 0)
(−6, 0, 6)
(−10, 2, −5)
(4, −9)
(9, −6, 7)
(5, −2, −6)
(7, −4)
(12, −19)
(1, −5, 3)

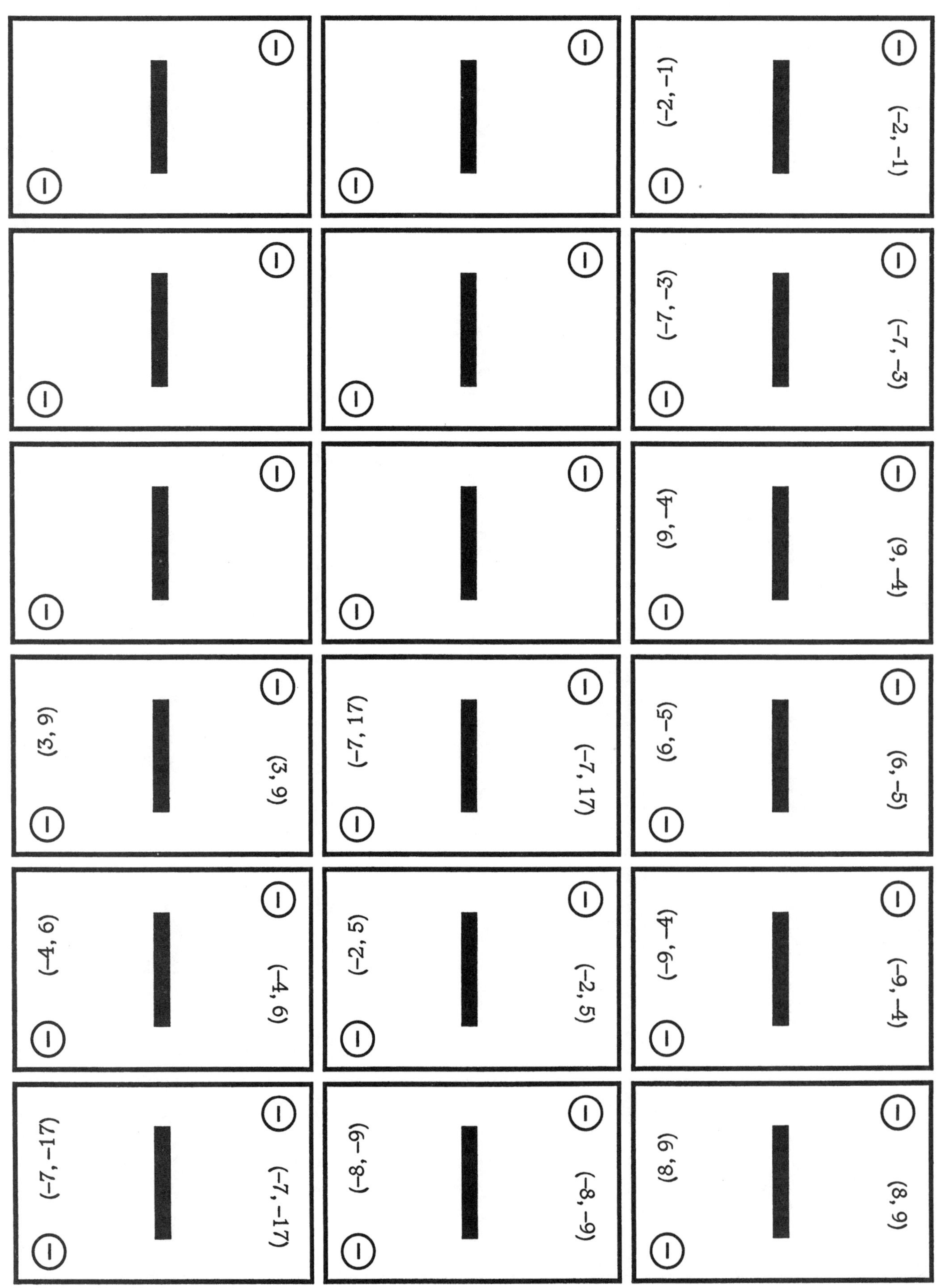

(−2, −1)
(−2, −1)
(−7, −3)
(−7, −3)
(9, −4)
(9, −4)
(3, 9)
(3, 9)
(−7, 17)
(−7, 17)
(6, −5)
(6, −5)
(−4, 6)
(−4, 6)
(−2, 5)
(−2, 5)
(−9, −4)
(−9, −4)
(−7, −17)
(−7, −17)
(−8, −9)
(−8, −9)
(8, 9)
(8, 9)

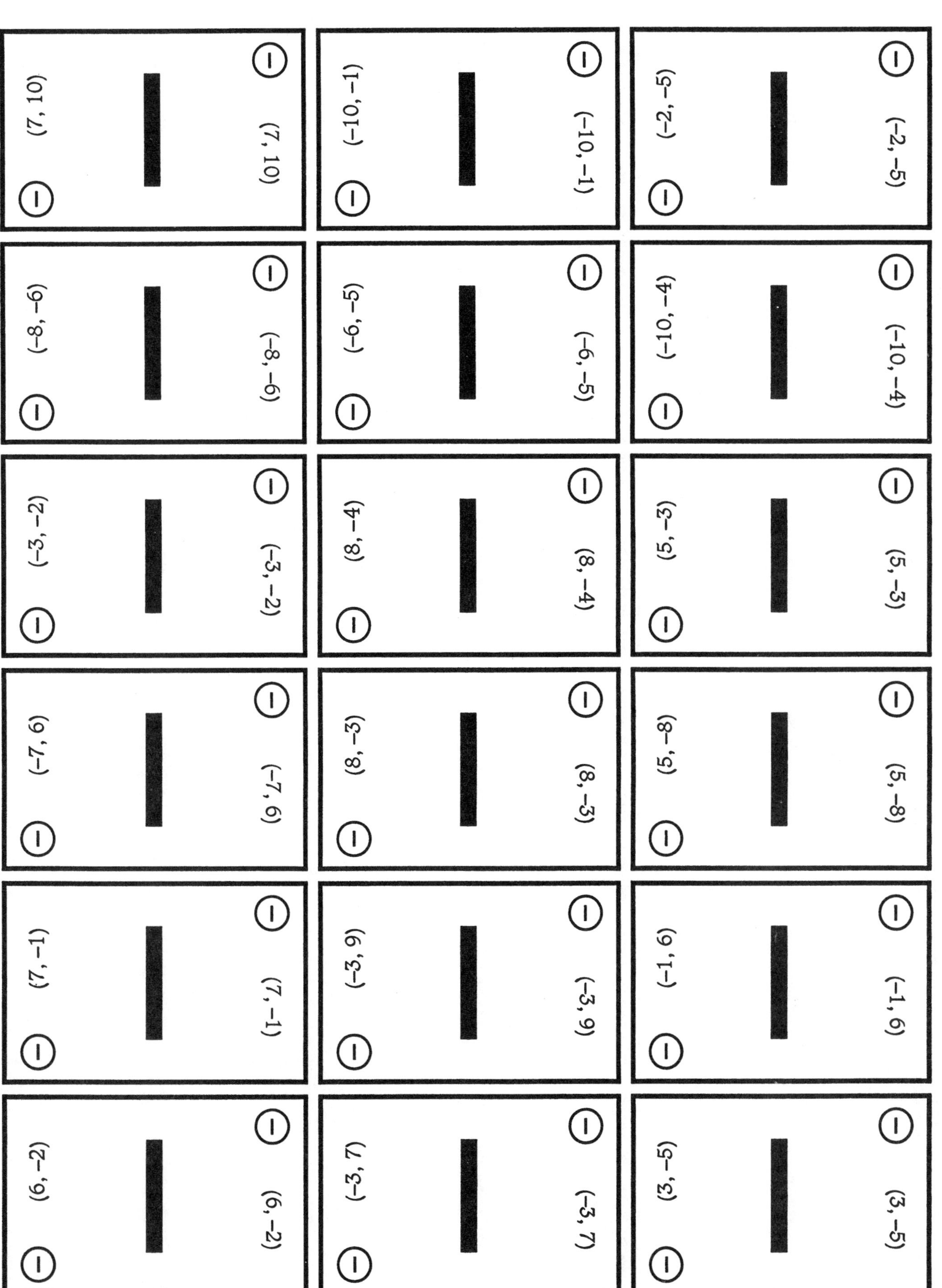
(7, 10)
(7, 10)
(−10, −1)
(−10, −1)
(−2, −5)
(−2, −5)
(−8, −6)
(−8, −6)
(−6, −5)
(−6, −5)
(−10, −4)
(−10, −4)
(−3, −2)
(−3, −2)
(8, −4)
(8, −4)
(5, −3)
(5, −3)
(−7, 6)
(−7, 6)
(8, −3)
(8, −3)
(5, −8)
(5, −8)
(7, −1)
(7, −1)
(−3, 9)
(−3, 9)
(−1, 6)
(−1, 6)
(6, −2)
(6, −2)
(−3, 7)
(−3, 7)
(3, −5)
(3, −5)

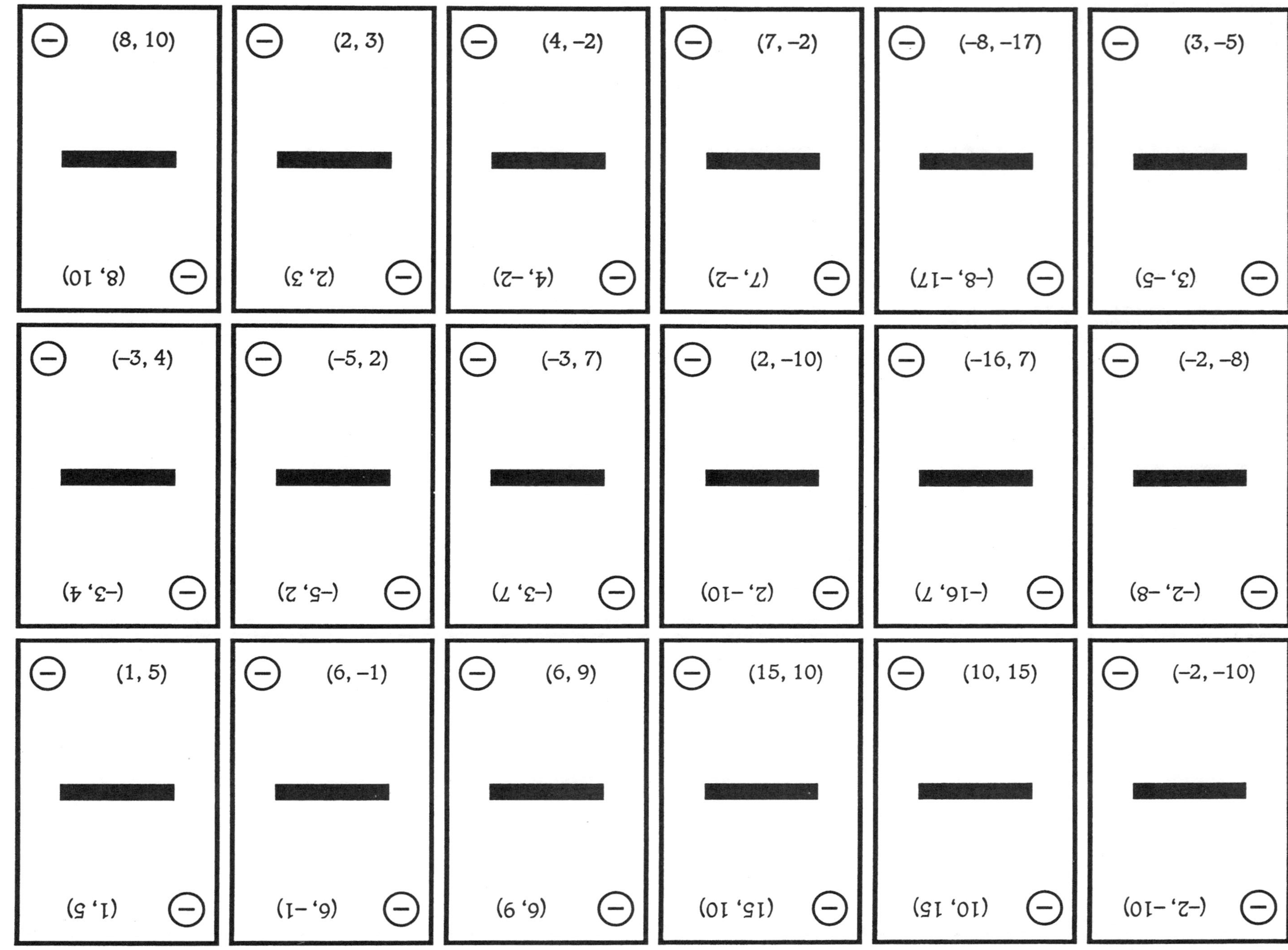
(8, 10)
(8, 10)
(2, 3)
(2, 3)
(4, −2)
(4, −2)
(7, −2)
(7, −2)
(−8, −17)
(−8, −17)
(3, −5)
(3, −5)
(−3, 4)
(−3, 4)
(−5, 2)
(−5, 2)
(−3, 7)
(−3, 7)
(2, −10)
(2, −10)
(−16, 7)
(−16, 7)
(−2, −8)
(−2, −8)
(1, 5)
(1, 5)
(6, −1)
(6, −1)
(6, 9)
(6, 9)
(15, 10)
(15, 10)
(10, 15)
(10, 15)
(−2, −10)
(−2, −10)

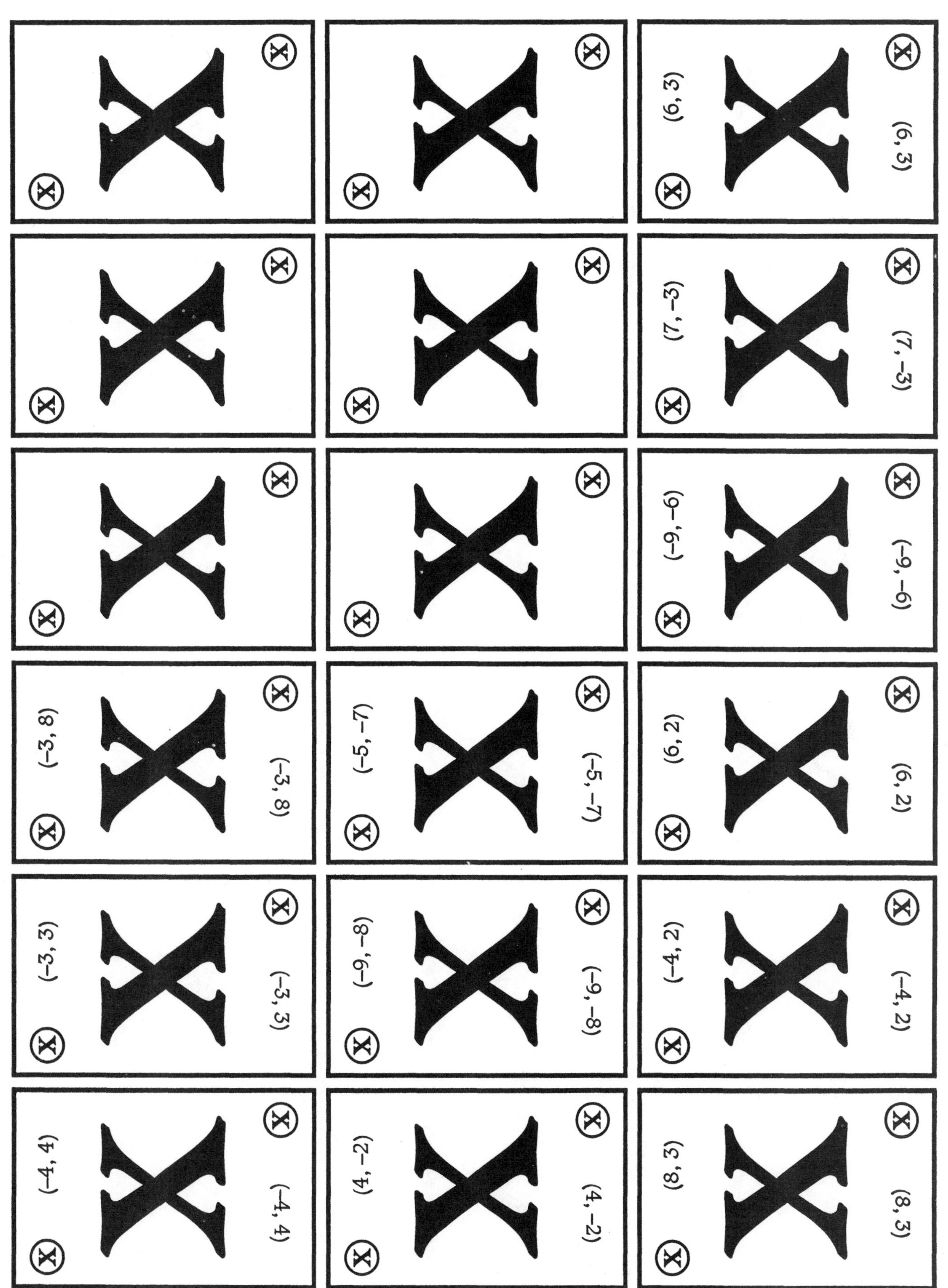
(6, 3)
(6, 3)
(7, –3)
(7, –3)
(–9, –6)
(–9, –6)
(–3, 8)
(–3, 8)
(–5, –7)
(–5, –7)
(6, 2)
(6, 2)
(–3, 3)
(–3, 3)
(–9, –8)
(–9, –8)
(–4, 2)
(–4, 2)
(–4, 4)
(–4, 4)
(4, –2)
(4, –2)
(8, 3)
(8, 3)

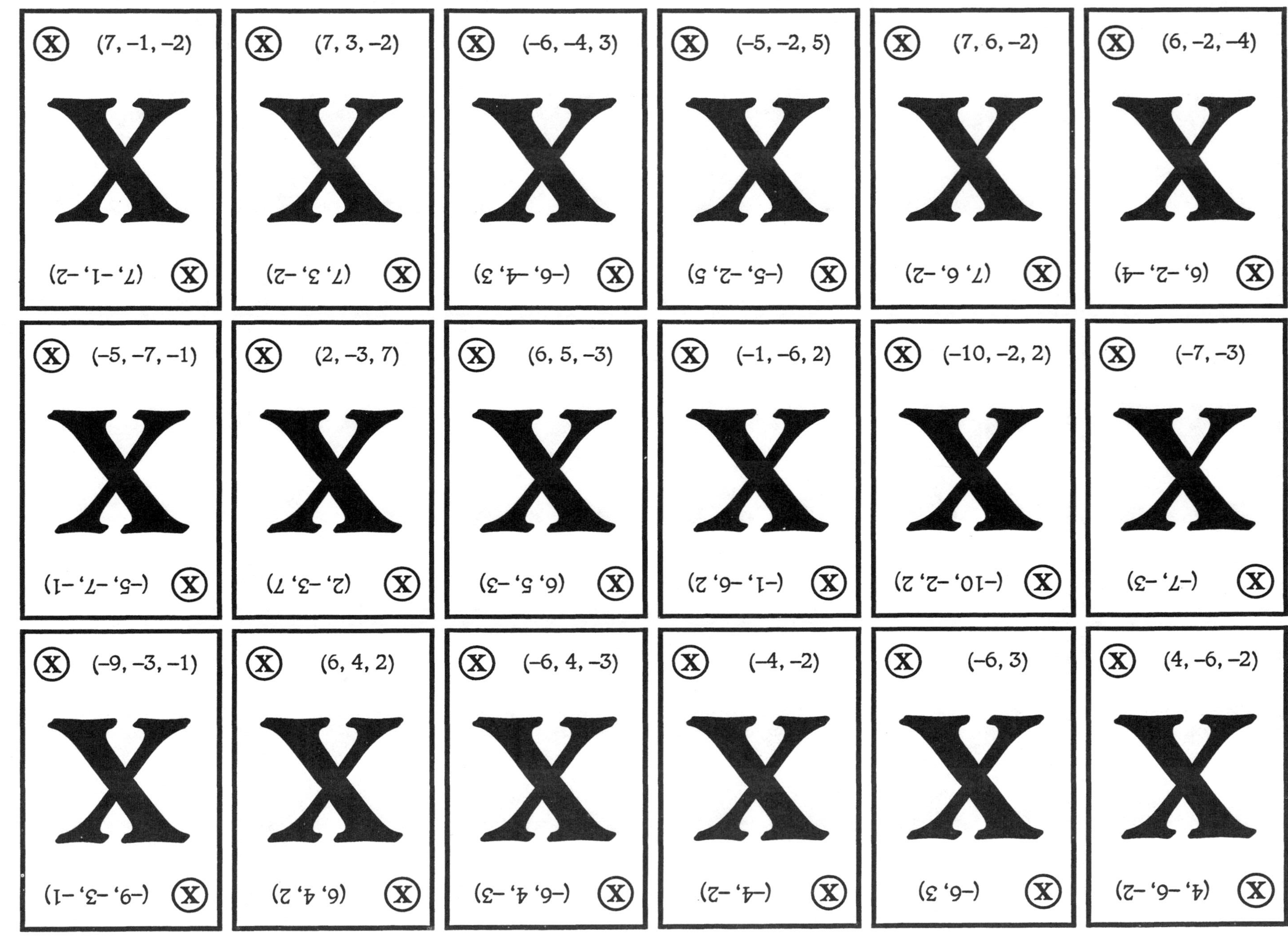
(7, –1, –2)
(7, 3, –2)
(–6, –4, 3)
(–5, –2, 5)
(7, 6, –2)
(6, –2, –4)
(–5, –7, –1)
(2, –3, 7)
(6, 5, –3)
(–1, –6, 2)
(–10, –2, 2)
(–7, –3)
(–9, –3, –1)
(6, 4, 2)
(–6, 4, –3)
(–4, –2)
(–6, 3)
(4, –6, –2)

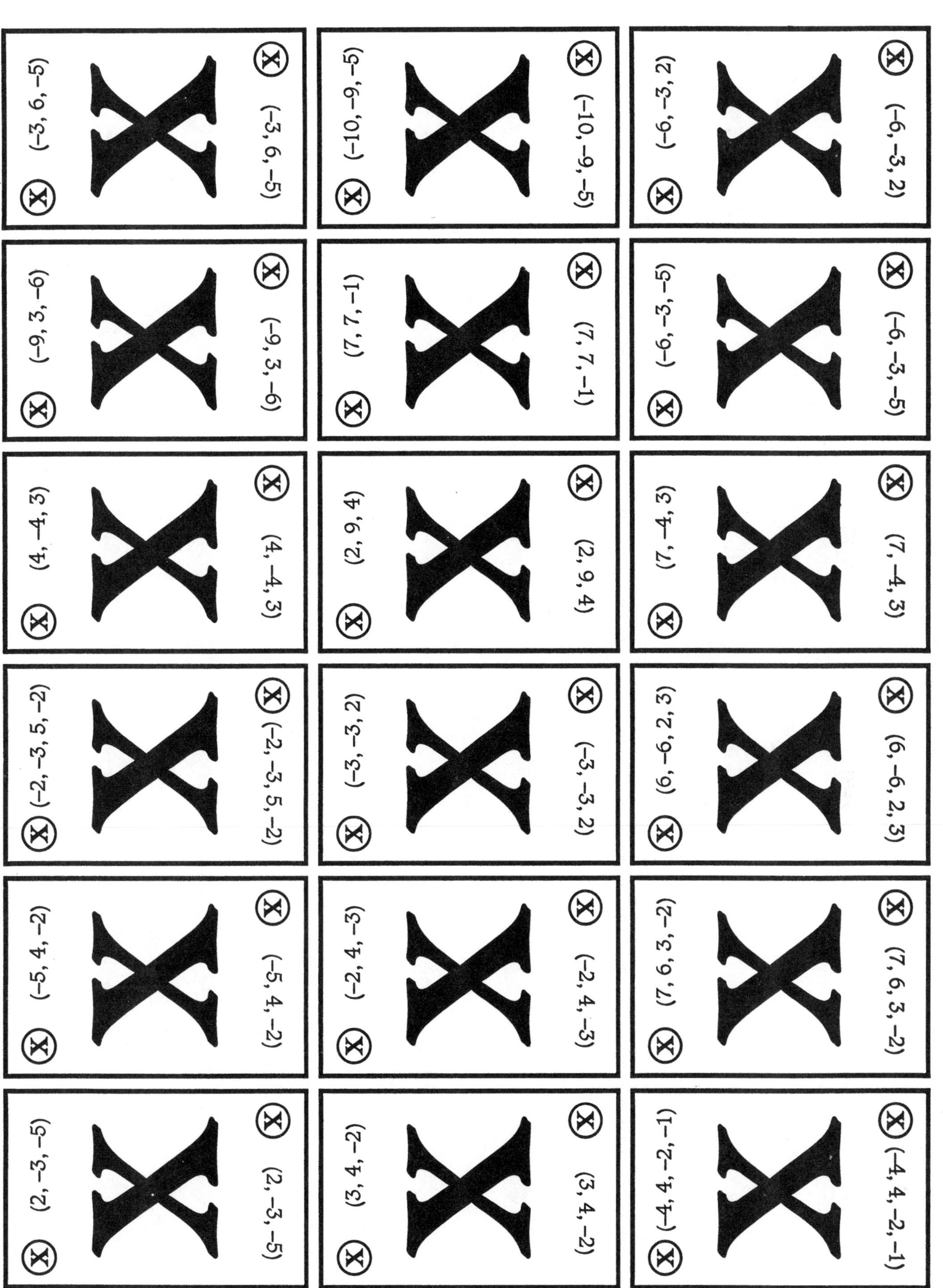

X
(−3, 6, −5)
X
(−10, −9, −5)
X
(−6, −3, 2)
X
(−9, 3, −6)
X
(7, 7, −1)
X
(−6, −3, −5)
X
(4, −4, 3)
X
(2, 9, 4)
X
(7, −4, 3)
X
(−2, −3, 5, −2)
X
(−3, −3, 2)
X
(6, −6, 2, 3)
X
(−5, 4, −2)
X
(−2, 4, −3)
X
(7, 6, 3, −2)
X
(2, −3, −5)
X
(3, 4, −2)
X
(−4, 4, −2, −1)

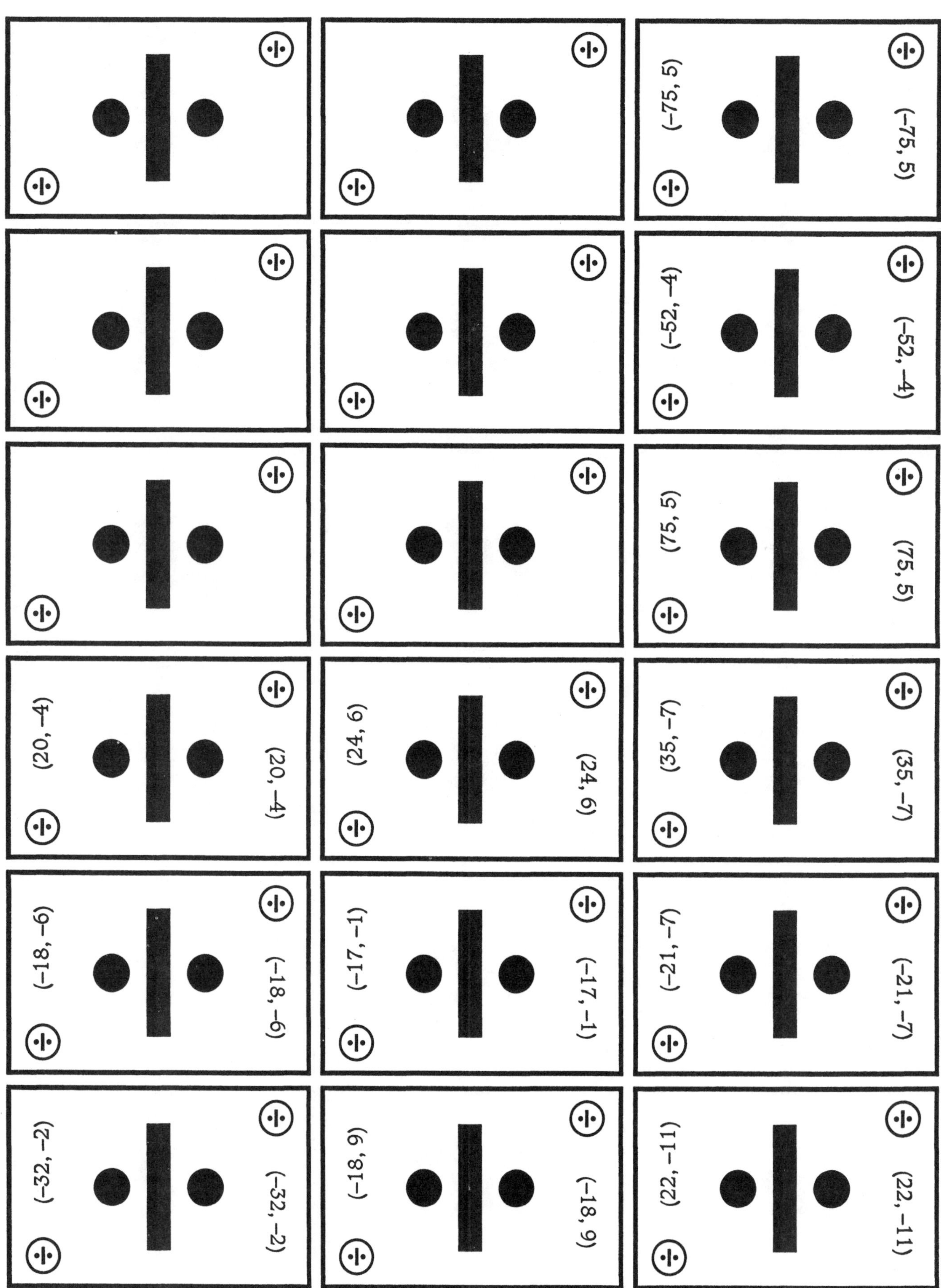
(−75, 5)
(−75, 5)
(−52, −4)
(−52, −4)
(75, 5)
(75, 5)
(20, −4)
(20, −4)
(24, 6)
(24, 6)
(35, −7)
(35, −7)
(−18, −6)
(−18, −6)
(−17, −1)
(−17, −1)
(−21, −7)
(−21, −7)
(−32, −2)
(−32, −2)
(−18, 9)
(−18, 9)
(22, −11)
(22, −11)

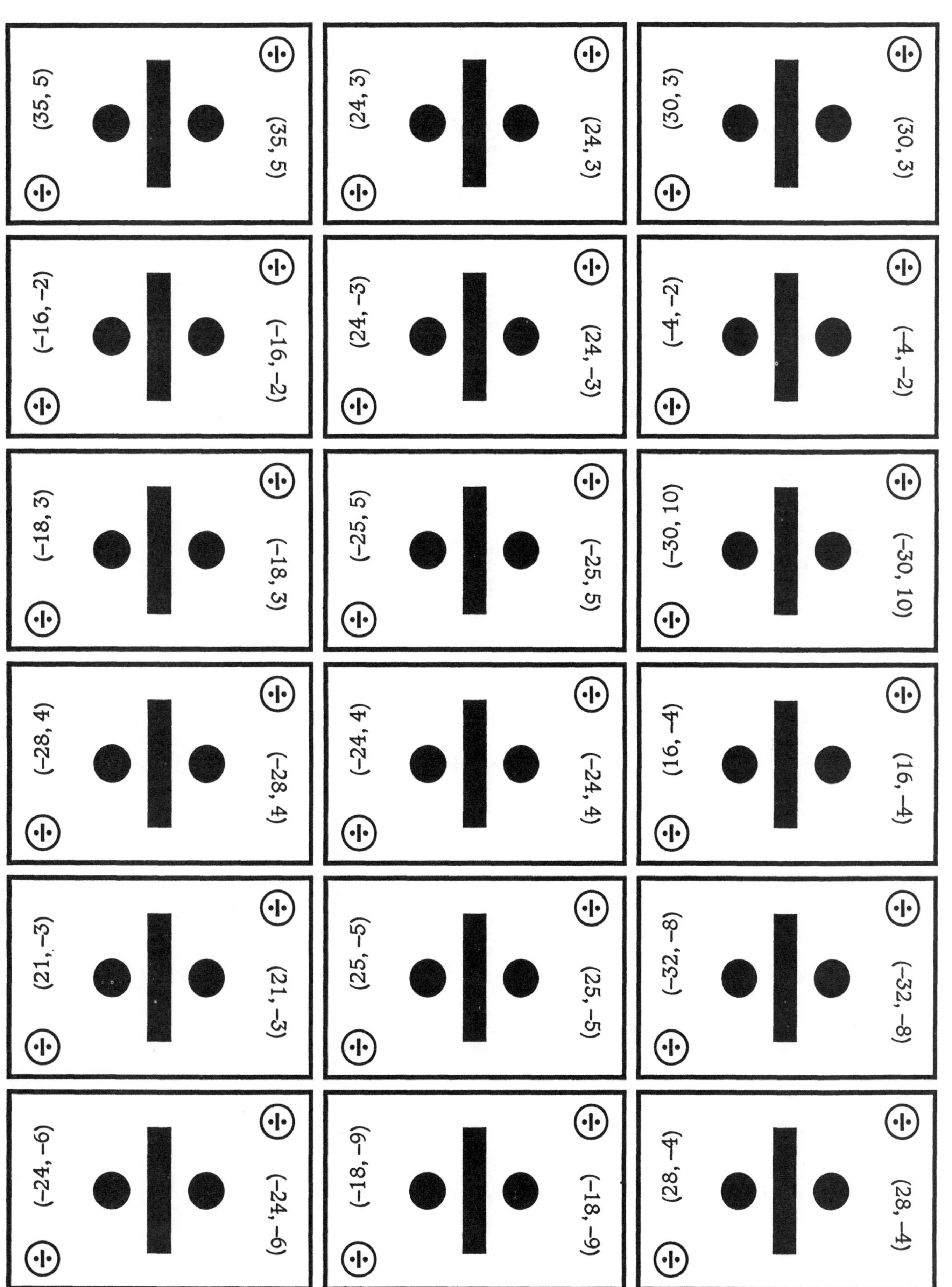
(35, 5)
(24, 3)
(30, 3)
(−16, −2)
(24, −3)
(−4, −2)
(−18, 3)
(−25, 5)
(−30, 10)
(−28, 4)
(−24, 4)
(16, −4)
(21, −3)
(25, −5)
(−32, −8)
(−24, −6)
(−18, −9)
(28, −4)

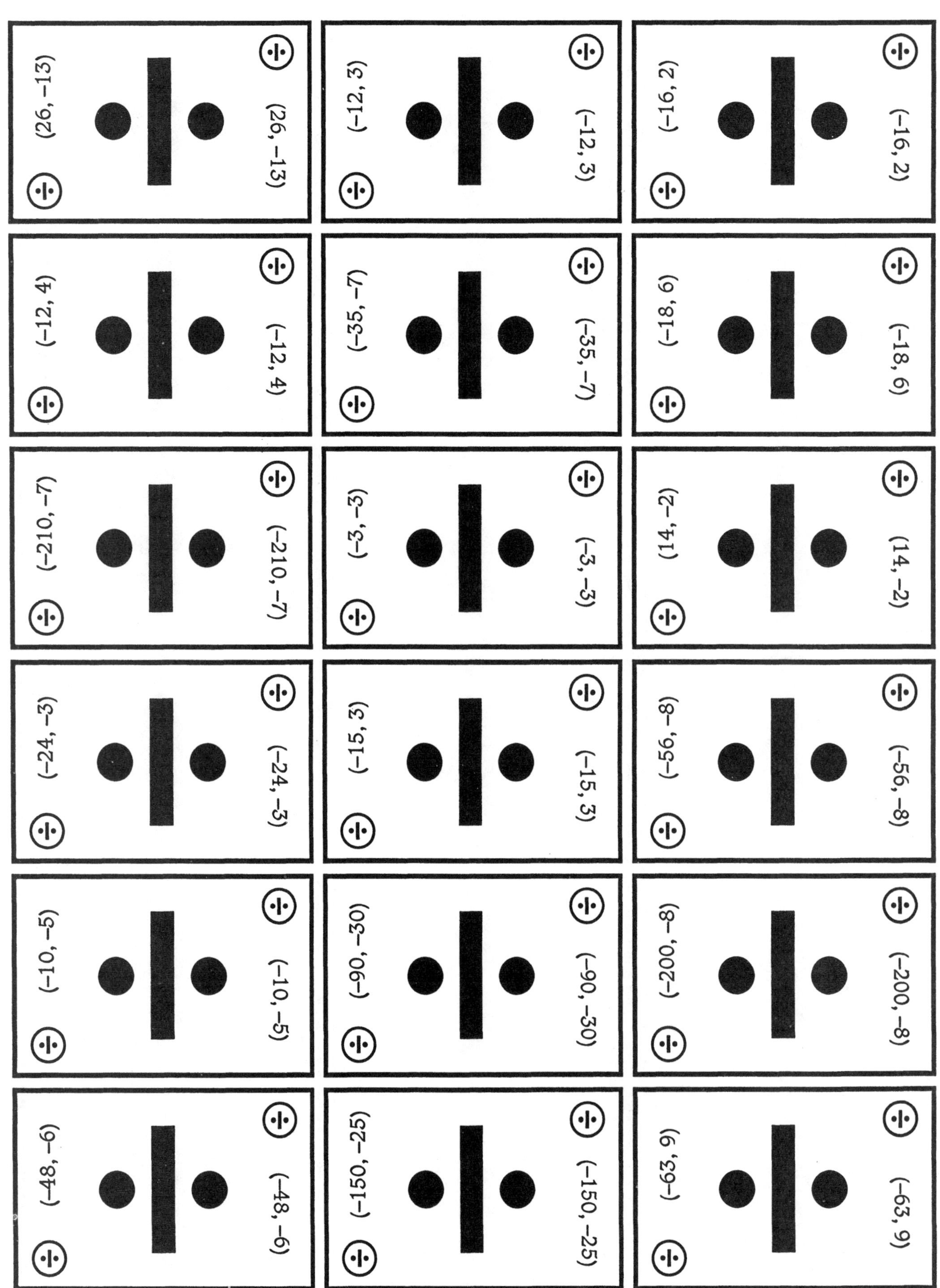
(26, −13)
(26, −13)
(−12, 3)
(−12, 3)
(−16, 2)
(−16, 2)
(−12, 4)
(−12, 4)
(−35, −7)
(−35, −7)
(−18, 6)
(−18, 6)
(−210, −7)
(−210, −7)
(−3, −3)
(−3, −3)
(14, −2)
(14, −2)
(−24, −3)
(−24, −3)
(−15, 3)
(−15, 3)
(−56, −8)
(−56, −8)
(−10, −5)
(−10, −5)
(−90, −30)
(−90, −30)
(−200, −8)
(−200, −8)
(−48, −6)
(−48, −6)
(−150, −25)
(−150, −25)
(−63, 9)
(−63, 9)

NEVER FORGET THE RULES OF INTEGERS

Elmo the Elephant has designed a game to reinforce the rules of integers in an exciting way.

Divide the class into two teams. Alternating turns, a player from each team selects an ordered pair card (patterns, page 78) and completes each step listed on the response card. Individual copies of the response cards are found below. When time is called, the team member must come to the board and write the answers. The opposing team can challenge the answers if they feel any one of the responses is incorrect. If the challenging team is correct, they receive double the point value for that category. If the challenging team is incorrect, they lose three points for each category challenged.

Each player responds to the category in the following manner:

Ordered Pair	(x, y)	(8, –4)
Add	(x + y)	(8) + (–4) = 4
Subtract	(x – y)	(8) – (–4) = 12
Multiply	(xy)	(8)(–4) = –32
Divide	x/y	8/–4 = –2
Total		(4) + (12) +(–32) + (–2) = –18

Each player earns the following points for each category:

Add (2.5 points) Subtract (2.5 points) Multiply (2.5 points) Divide (2.5 points) Total (5 points)

RESPONSE CARDS

Ordered Pair	(________)
Add	________
Subtract	________
Multiply	________
Divide	________
Total	________

Ordered Pair	(________)
Add	________
Subtract	________
Multiply	________
Divide	________
Total	________

Ordered Pair	(________)
Add	________
Subtract	________
Multiply	________
Divide	________
Total	________

Ordered Pair	(________)
Add	________
Subtract	________
Multiply	________
Divide	________
Total	________

Ordered Pair Cards

(–8, 4)	(–12, –4)	(–6, –2)	(–6, 3)
(15, –5)	(–12, –12)	(–12, 3)	(16, 8)
(–9, –3)	(9, –3)	(–11, –11)	(–10, –2)
(10, –2)	(–10, 2)	(–12, –6)	(12, –6)
(–14, –7)	(14, 7)	(14, –7)	(–14, 7)
(10, 5)	(–10, –5)	(–10, 5)	(10, –5)
(4, –2)	(–4, –2)	(4, 2)	(–4, 2)
(25, 5)	(25, –5)	(–25, –5)	(–25, 5)
(15, 3)	(15, –3)	(–15, 3)	(–15, –3)

TIC–TAC–FIVE IN A ROW

Number of Players: Groups of two

Materials:
- Twenty–five index cards
- Pencil
- One answer grid per player
- Game pieces (pennies, small pieces of paper, etc.)

To Play:

1. Write one equation from the list below on each index card, shuffle all of the cards, and place them face down in a pile.
2. Players take turns drawing a card and solving the equations.
3. If the answer is correct, players place a game piece on the matching square on the answer grid.
4. The first player to place five game pieces in a row, either horizontally, vertically, or diagonally, wins the game.

Equations:

1. $2x - 3x - 2 = -7$
2. $5x + 3 = 2x + 21$
3. $3x + 1 = x + 19$
4. $2(3x + 4) = -10$
5. $2x + 10 + x = 4x + 9$
6. $4x - 2x + 3 = 2x + x - 2x - 1$
7. $4x + 9 = 17$
8. $-(3x - 3) = -9$
9. $2(2x + 2) = 6x + 8$
10. $3(x + 4) = 21$
11. $9x = 7x + 14$
12. $3x - 1 = x - 13$
13. $3x + x - 2x + 4 = 26$
14. $4x + 14 = -10 + 2x + 10$
15. $2(2x + 15) = -x - 10$
16. $4(x - 1) = -x - 29$
17. $4x = 2x + 16$
18. $4x - 5 = 5x + 12$
19. $5(x + 4) = 3(x - 2)$
20. $-7x + 5x = 0$
21. $x - 13 - x + 2x = 21$
22. $2(x - 4) - 16 = 0$
23. $5x + 14 = 2x - 19$
24. $11x + 2(x + 6) = -1$
25. $0.1x - 2.5x + 2 = 50$

Answer Grid

5	1	2	7	–3
–2	–6	–4	11	–7
–8	3	6	8	–17
9	–5	–13	4	12
0	17	–11	–1	–20

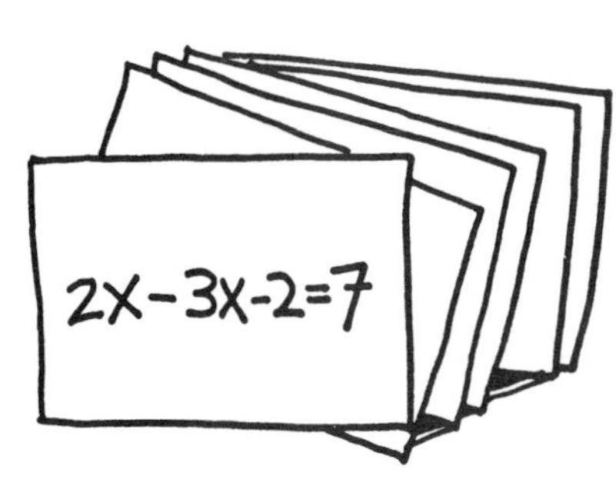

"Boning Up" On Solving Equations

Students come into the classroom with many false impressions that are counter-productive to their success in school. One of the most damaging is: "I can't do math!" Another is: "Solving equations is like performing magic."

"Boning Up" on Solving Equations was designed to improve students' attitudes while developing their equation–solving skills. The activity is challenging and fun to complete. It is also a versatile activity: teachers can design game pieces to fit the skill level of their individual students. Once the game pieces have been designed, using the pattern below, the teacher has a valuable resource that can be used at any time to reinforce math skills.

Write an equation on each bone. Students will attempt to solve these problems to win the game. This game is designed for either groups of two students each or two groups of half the class each.

To Play:

1. Give each group a set of bones, a game board, and one die.
2. Place the bones face down on the table.
3. Each player takes a turn selecting the bone on the top of the stack and solving the problem. If the problem is solved correctly, the player rolls a die to determine the number of spaces he or she will move on the game board. Watch out! Don't end up in the dog pound. If a player ends up on the square that states "the dog pound," he or she must roll an even number to get out on his or her next turn. If the problem is answered incorrectly, the player loses a turn. A scientific calculator can be used to check the answers.
4. Players progress around the game board, following the directions listed.
5. The first player to reach the dog house, without being thrown in the dog pound, is the winner.

"BONING UP" ON SOLVING EQUATIONS GAME BOARD

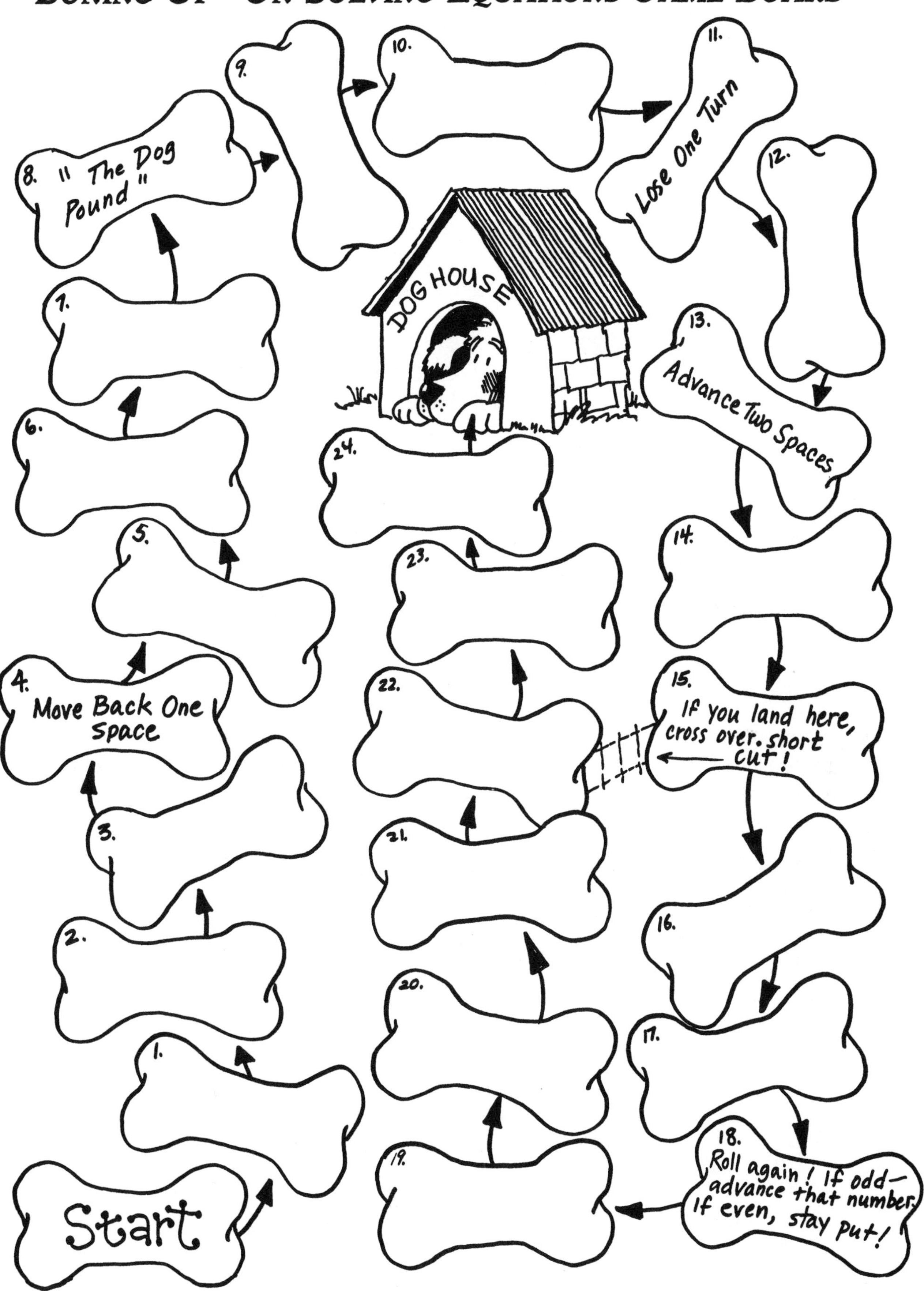

Coordinate Hangman

You have entered the Wild, Wild West, and finding your neck in a noose is a real possibility. The object of this game is to successfully identify the coordinates of a specific word before you lose the game and find your neck in the noose.

Materials:

• a coordinate grid • hangman position board • category list

This is a game for either two players or two teams.

To Play:

1. Player 1 chooses a category from the category list below. He or she must then think of a word from that category. For example, Player 1 selects the category Favorite Color and chooses the word "blue."
2. Player 1 records the category and the word on a sheet of paper out of the view of Player 2.
3. Player 1 then uses the Coordinate Grid (pattern, page 83) to locate the points of the letters in the word "blue" (for example, B[6, 4] L[–8, 5] U[4, –6] E[5, 8]). This information is also hidden from Player 2.
4. Player 1 tells Player 2 the chosen category and the number of letters in the word (for example, "Favorite Color, 4 letters").
5. Player 2 draws blank lines on a sheet of paper to represent the number of letters in the word.
6. Using a copy of the Coordinate Grid, Player 2 guesses one letter and names its coordinates. If this letter is in the word, Player 1 tells Player 2 to place the letter in a certain blank space. If the guess is incorrect, Player 1 tells Player 2 that the letter is not in the word.
7. Player 2 begins the game with 100 points. As indicated on the hangman Position Board (pattern, page 83), with each incorrect guess, the player loses 10 points. The pictures on the board show the player how close he or she is to being hanged.
8. The goal of the game is to guess the word before reaching 0 on the position board.
9. Each game consists of 10 rounds, with each player or team alternating the role of Writer and Guesser.
10. The player or team with the most points wins.

Category List

Name of a President	Favorite Food Item
Favorite Color	Geometric Shape
Favorite Pet	Mathematical Term
Favorite Ice Cream	

Coordinate Grid

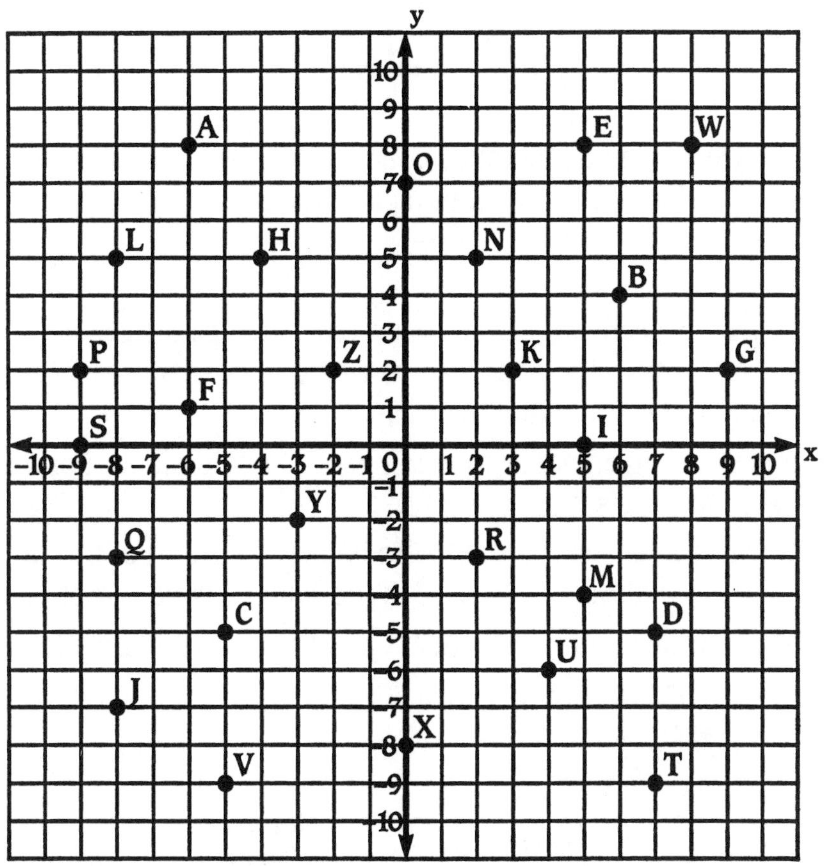

Hangman Position Board

I HAVE . . . WHO HAS . . . ?

A fun way to review basic mathematical facts is to play a game of "I Have . . . Who Has . . . ?" This particular version reviews square roots.

To Play:

1. Distribute all playing cards to the students (patterns, pages 85–86). This may require some students to have more than 1 card. Two blank cards are also provided so that you may write in additional problems.
2. The teacher calls on one student to read his or her card aloud. For example, "I Have 2. Who has the square root of 9?"
3. The student with the answer to the "Who has . . ." portion of the card reads his or her card aloud. For example, "I Have 3. Who has the square root of 25?"
4. This process continues until each student has read his or her card(s).
5. If all of the "Who has" portions were answered correctly, and all cards were read, the game was played correctly.

Note:

- The teacher will want to play the game until reading and responding to the cards becomes easy for the students. The teacher can then redistribute the cards and play again.

- Periodically, the teacher may want to use these cards as a brief review of the concept of square roots. Once the students understand the procedure of "I Have . . . Who Has?" the activity can be completed in less than five minutes.

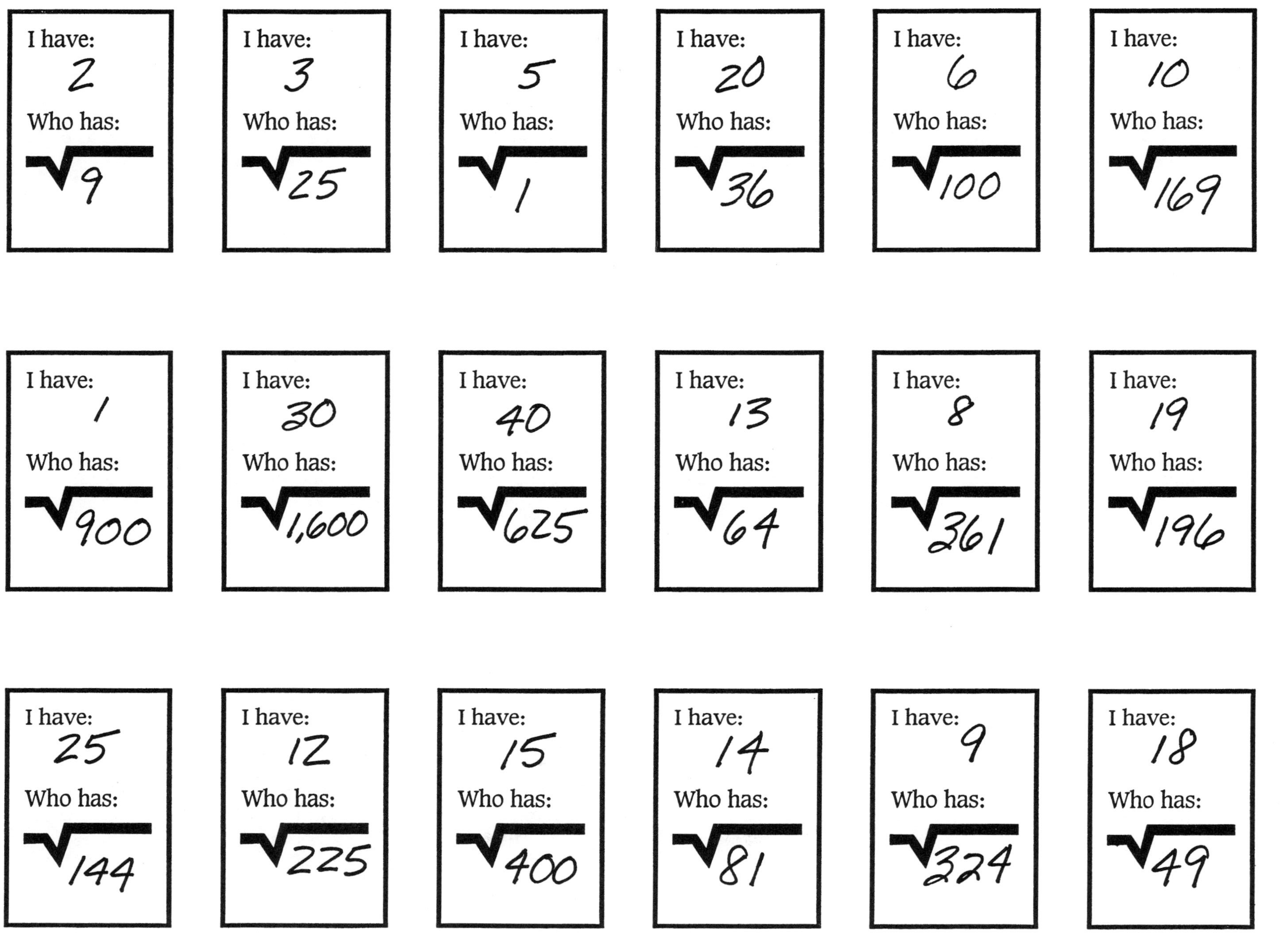
I have: 2 Who has: √9
I have: 3 Who has: √25
I have: 5 Who has: √1
I have: 20 Who has: √36
I have: 6 Who has: √100
I have: 10 Who has: √169
I have: 1 Who has: √900
I have: 30 Who has: √1,600
I have: 40 Who has: √625
I have: 13 Who has: √64
I have: 8 Who has: √361
I have: 19 Who has: √196
I have: 25 Who has: √144
I have: 12 Who has: √225
I have: 15 Who has: √400
I have: 14 Who has: √81
I have: 9 Who has: √324
I have: 18 Who has: √49

I have: 7 Who has: √121
I have: 11 Who has: √256
I have: 16 Who has: √289
I have: 22 Who has: √8,100
I have: 90 Who has: √529
I have: 23 Who has: √676
I have: 17 Who has: √10,000
I have: 100 Who has: √16
I have: 4 Who has: √441
I have: 26 Who has: √4,900
I have: 70 Who has: √576
I have: 24 Who has: √3,600
I have: 21 Who has: √2,500
I have: 50 Who has: √6,400
I have: 80 Who has: √484
I have: 60 Who has: √4
I have: Who has: √
I have: Who has: √

WHAT'S THE POINT?

There are times in math class when you may wonder, "What's the point?" Let's answer that question by getting to the point.

Point itself is an undefined term, but it helps define other geometric shapes. In this game, we will get to the point, but we must have two points to do so.

The object of the game is to identify the slope of a line given two points on the line. Don't forget the formula: **Slope =** $y_2 - y_1 / x_2 - x_1$

Even though a line consists of an infinite number of points, we need only two to be able to identify the slope.

Materials:

- Game board for each pair of students (page 88)
- Game pieces (pennies or scraps of paper, etc.)
- Index cards (to make letter cards)

To Play:

1. Students group themselves in pairs. Each pair needs a game board.
2. Alternating turns, each player chooses the letter on the game board that he or she would like to identify, draws that letter card, and tries to identify the slope of the line given the two points listed on the card. If identified correctly, the player covers the letter on the board with a game piece. Each player tries to capture five squares in a row, either horizontally, vertically, or diagonally.
3. The next player strategically decides which letter to attempt. If a player answers incorrectly, a turn is lost.
4. The winner is the first player to cover five squares in a row, either horizontally, vertically, or diagonally.

Write the letter card information on one side of each index card. Label each card with a letter of the alphabet. Write the answer (the slope) on the back of each card, so that students may check to see if their answers are correct.

Letter Cards		Slope	Letter Cards		Slope
A	(2, 3) (1,5)	–2	N	(–1, –2) (0, 3)	5
B	(–3, 2) (1,5)	3/4	O	(–2, 0) (2, –3)	–3/4
C	(2, 3) (2, 5)	undefined slope	P	(3, 0) (–2, 5)	–1
D	(2, 5) (–2, 5)	0	Q	(8, 1) (–8, –3)	1/4
E	(1, –1) (5, 6)	7/4	R	(0, 7) (–2, –5)	6
F	(4, 0) (–1, 2)	–2/5	S	(–1, –2) (0, 0)	2
G	(4, 1) (–3, 1)	0	T	(9, 5) (7, 6)	–1/2
H	(–1, 2) (4, 7)	1	U	(2, –4) (5, –6)	–2/3
I	(3, 4) (2, 6)	–2	V	(–8, 1) (–6, 3)	1
J	(7, 1) (3, 2)	–1/4	W	(–6, –7) (–4, –4)	3/2
K	(3, –1), (6, 7)	8/3	X	(2, 7) (4, 3)	–2
L	(–3, –1) (1, –4)	–3/4	Y	(–5, 3) (6, 5)	2/11
M	(0, –1), (1, 4)	5			

What's The Point?

K	D	W	E	C
B	U	J	P	Y
G	X	A	T	L
S	Q	V	N	H
O	M	F	I	R

Geometric Ski Resort

Win a trip to a famous ski resort—all expenses paid!

At most ski resorts, vacationers can't wait to feel the wind hit their faces as they slide effortlessly down the slopes. The Geometric Ski Resort, however, has other kinds of slopes in mind. The vacationer is spared the cost of an expensive snowsuit, head gear, and skiis. To have fun on the slopes at this resort, the vacationer must *find* the slopes first. The participant must identify the slope and y–intercept given the equation of a line.

Materials (for each group):

- One game board displaying slopes and y–intercepts (page 90)
- A deck of linear equation cards (see equations below)
- One die
- Game pieces (small pieces of paper, pennies, etc.)

To Play:

1. Each participant rolls the die to determine the first player (high score).
2. Alternating turns, each player chooses a card from the deck and identifies the slope and y–intercept.
3. The player then finds the answer on the game board and covers it with his or her game piece.
4. If answered incorrectly, the player loses a turn.
5. The winner is the first player to capture five game pieces in a row, either vertically, horizontally, or diagonally.

Write the following equations on index cards. On one side of the card write the equation, and on the other side of the card, write the slope and y–intercepts. After the student has identified the slope and y–intercept, he or she may turn the card over to check the answer.

Equation Cards	Slope & Y–Intercepts		Equation Cards	Slope & Y–Intercepts	
$-3x + y = 2$	$m = 3$	$b = 2$	$y = 15$	$m = 0$	$b = 15$
$3x - y = 0$	$m = 3$	$b = 0$	$21x + 10y = -4$	$m = -2.1$	$b = -0.4$
$2x + y = -1$	$m = -2$	$b = -1$	$18x - 10y = 25$	$m = 1.8$	$b = -2.5$
$x + y = 7$	$m = -1$	$b = 7$	$x + y = 5$	$m = -1$	$b = 5$
$6x - 3y = -1$	$m = 2$	$b = 1/3$	$2x - y = -3$	$m = 2$	$b = 3$
$9x + 3y = 2$	$m = -3$	$b = 2/3$	$x - y = 4$	$m = -1$	$b = -4$
$x - 5y = -20$	$m = 1/5$	$b = 4$	$-x + 3y = 9$	$m = 1/3$	$b = 3$
$3x + 4y = 8$	$m = -3/4$	$b = 2$	$x - 2y = 6$	$m = 1/2$	$b = -3$
$-30x + 5y = -3$	$m = 6$	$b = -3/5$	$2x - y = -7$	$m = 2$	$b = 7$
$2x + 3y = -3$	$m = -2/3$	$b = -1$	$4x - y = -11$	$m = 4$	$b = 11$
$14x - 6y = 1$	$m = 7/3$	$b = -1/6$	$3x + y = 18$	$m = -3$	$b = 18$
$10x + 8y = -7$	$m = -5/4$	$b = -7/8$	$2x + y = 5$	$m = -2$	$b = 5$
$y = -6$	$m = 0$	$b = -6$			

Linear Equation Game Board

$m = 1.8$ $b = -2.5$	$m = -1$ $b = -4$	$m = -3$ $b = 2/3$	$m = 0$ $b = 15$	$m = -2$ $b = 5$
$m = -1$ $b = 5$	$m = 6$ $b = -3/5$	$m = 1/3$ $b = 3$	$m = -3/4$ $b = 2$	$m = -2/3$ $b = -1$
$m = 2$ $b = 1/3$	$m = 2$ $b = 3$	$m = 7/3$ $b = -1/6$	$m = -2.1$ $b = -0.4$	$m = 3$ $b = 2$
$m = -3$ $b = 18$	$m = 0$ $b = -6$	$m = 4$ $b = 11$	$m = -1$ $b = 7$	$m = 1/2$ $b = -3$
$m = 1/5$ $b = 4$	$m = -5/4$ $b = -7/8$	$m = -2$ $b = -1$	$m = 3$ $b = 0$	$m = 2$ $b = 7$

WHAT'S MY LINE?

Today, people may try to give us different "lines," but there is one geometric fact that always holds true: "Between any two points there is just one line." With that in mind, each participant will be given two points or the slope and y–intercept to determine the equation of the line. The game is designed for two players per board.

Materials:

• Game board (page 92) • Game pieces (pieces of paper, pennies, etc.)

• One die • One deck of equation cards (see equations below)

To Play:

1. Each participant rolls the die to determine the first player (high score).
2. Alternating turns, each player picks the first card in the deck and uses the given points or slope and y–intercept to write the equation in standard form. The player then finds the matching equation on the game board and covers it with his or her game piece.
3. If answered incorrectly, the participant loses a turn. The participants should make sure that the cards are stacked properly, as the answers are listed on the back side of the cards. Used cards are placed in a discard pile.
4. The winner is the first player to capture five squares in a row, either diagonally, horizontally, or vertically. If there is no winner, the cards are reshuffled to create a new draw pile.

Write the following points or slope and y–intercept pairs on index cards, one per card. On the back of each card, write the matching equation. After the student has written the equation, the card may be turned over to verify the answer.

Points/Slope and Y–Intercept	Equations	Points/Slope and Y–Intercept	Equations
(3, 13) (–4, –22)	$5x - y = 2$	$m = -1$ $b = 5$	$x + y = 5$
(0, –2) (3, 7)	$3x - y = 2$	$m = 2$ $b = 3$	$2x - y = -3$
(–2, 14) (0, 8)	$3x + y = 8$	$m = 1$ $b = -4$	$x - y = 4$
(2, 0) (0, 4)	$2x + y = 4$	$m = 1/3$ $b = 3$	$-x + 3y = 9$
(–2, –9) (3, –4)	$x - y = 7$	$m = 1/2$ $b = -3$	$x - 2y = 6$
(3, –1) (4, 4)	$5x - y = 16$	$m = 3/2$ $b = -3$	$-3x + 2y = -6$
(6, 0) (–9, 10)	$2x + 3y = 12$	$m = -2/3$ $b = 0$	$2x + 3y = 0$
(0, 12) (9, 0)	$4x + 3y = 36$	$m = 4/3$ $b = -4$	$4x - 3y = 12$
(0, –8) (3, 0)	$8x - 3y = 24$	$m = 4/5$ $b = 3$	$-4x + 5y = 15$
(10, –4) (5, 0)	$4x + 5y = 20$	$m = 5/2$ $b = 0$	$5x - 2y = 0$
(–8, –15) (–2, –6)	$3x - 2y = 6$	$m = 2$ $b = -6$	$2x - y = 6$
$m = -3/4$ $b = 9$	$3x + 4y = 36$	$m = 3/4$ $b = 2$	$-3x + 4y = 8$
$m = 2/3$ $b = -2$	$2x - 3y = 6$		

WHAT'S MY LINE GAME BOARD

$5x - y = 2$	$3x - y = 2$	$3x + y = 8$	$2x + y = 4$	$x - y = 7$
$5x - y = 16$	$2x + 3y = 12$	$4x + 3y = 36$	$8x - 3y = 24$	$4x + 5y = 20$
$3x - 2y = 6$	$3x + 4y = 36$	$2x - 3y = 6$	$x + y = 5$	$2x - y = -3$
$x - y = 4$	$-x + 3y = 9$	$x - 2y = 6$	$-3x + 2y = -6$	$2x + 3y = 0$
$4x - 3y = 12$	$-4x + 5y = 15$	$5x - 2y = 0$	$2x - y = 6$	$-3x + 4y = 8$

It's Exponent To Get Five In A Row!

Number of Players:

- Groups of two

Materials:

- Twenty–five index cards
- Pencil
- One answer grid per player
- Game pieces (small pieces of paper, pennies, etc.)

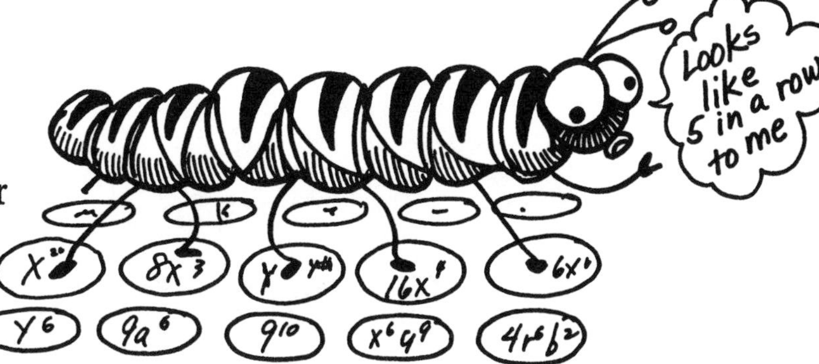

To Play:

1. Write one exponential expression from the list below on each index card, shuffle all of the cards, and place them face down in a pile.
2. The players take turns drawing a card from the pile and simplifying the exponential expression.
3. Once the answer is in its simplest form, the players place a game piece on the matching square on the answer grid.
4. The first player to place five game pieces in a row, either horizontally, vertically, or diagonally, wins the game.

Exponential Expressions

1. $(y^3)(y^3)$	6. $2(x)^4$	11. $(x^a)^2$	16. $(3xy^5)^4$	21. $(x^5)(x^3)$
2. $(y^2)^4$	7. $(a^5)^2$	12. $(x^a)(x^2)$	17. $(9x^2y^2)(9x^2y^{10})$	22. $(3x^2)(2y^2)$
3. $(x^2y^3)^3$	8. $(a^5)(a^2)$	13. $(3a^3)(3a^3)$	18. $(2r^3b)^2$	23. $(3xy)^2$
4. $(2x)(2x)(2x)$	9. $(y^x)(y^x)(y^x)$	14. $(3a^3)^3$	19. $(2br^2)(r)(2rb)$	24. $(x^0)(x)(x^2)(x^3)$
5. $(2x)^4$	10. $(y^x)^4$	15. $(b^5)(c^4)$	20. $(x^5)^3$	25. $(4x^0)(4x^2)$

Answer Grid

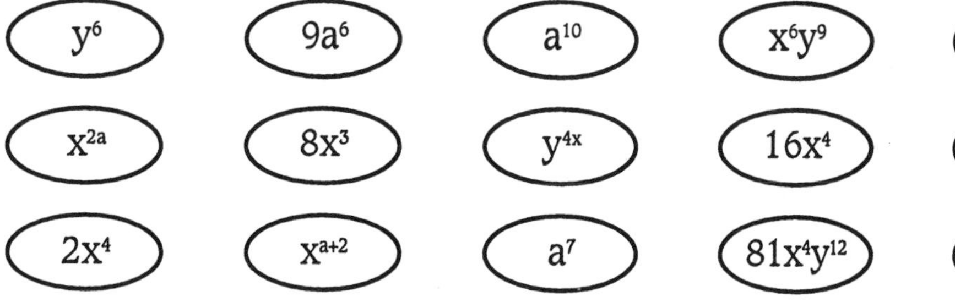

y^6	$9a^6$	a^{10}	x^6y^9	$4r^6b^2$
x^{2a}	$8x^3$	y^{4x}	$16x^4$	$6x^2y^2$
$2x^4$	x^{a+2}	a^7	$81x^4y^{12}$	y^{3x}
$27a^9$	$4r^4b^2$	b^5c^4	x^{15}	x^6
$81x^4y^{20}$	x^8	$9x^2y^2$	$16x^2$	y^8

Part Three:

GEOMETRY READINESS

Is It Probability Or Is It Probably Not?

Challenge a friend to the following game. Tell your friend that you have magical powers. You can add the numbers on the top of the dice plus the numbers on the bottom of the dice without even seeing them!

Select five dice. Since you are so smart, inform your friend that you believe you can add the top numbers and the bottom numbers (that you can't see) on the five dice faster than he or she can add just the top numbers.

Roll all five dice. Quickly shout out, "35." (Your friend will be amazed!)

Verify your answer by counting aloud the top numbers, and then flip over the dice and add the bottom numbers.

To further amaze your friend, select seven dice. Make the same challenge as before. Tell your friend that you will be able to add the top and the bottom numbers quicker than he or she can add the top numbers.

Roll all seven dice. Quickly shout out, "49." (Your friend will faint!)

Verify your answer by counting aloud the top numbers, and then turn over the dice and add the bottom numbers.

Finally, challenge your friend by stating that you can do this trick with ten dice.

Roll all ten dice. Quickly shout out, "70." You are amazing!

Write an explanation of how you accomplished this phenomenal feat.

____

____

____

____

____

____

____

____

____

____

Name ______________________________ Date ____________

Paper Folding And Protractors

One of the principal tools mathematicians use for measuring angles is the protractor. You can buy a protractor at the store, but perhaps making your own from a piece of paper will help you understand more about lines and angles.

Draw a circle with a diameter of between four and six inches. Cut out your circle.

- If a circle has a measurement of 360°, what do you think a half–circle will measure?

Fold your circle on one of its diameters. Using a straight edge and a pencil, draw a line on the diameter. Label this line AB.

- Is the diameter shown in the circle to the right the only diameter? Why or why not?

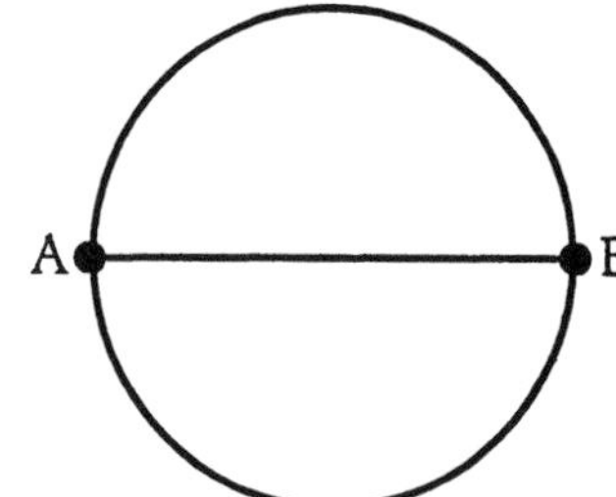

Cut your circle on the diameter. Discard one of the half–circles. Look at the remaining half–circle.

- Can you explain why it measures 180°? (Do not say that it's because a circle has a measurement of 360°, and a half–circle is half of that. That information was given above. There are other reasons.)

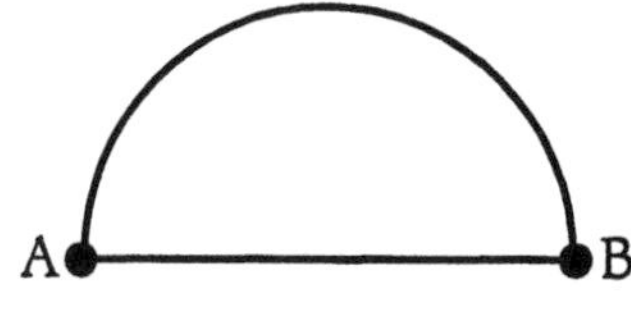

Fold your half–circle in half, as shown. Using a straight edge and a pencil, trace the fold line. Label this line CD.

- If the half–circle measured 180°, what do angle ACD and angle BCD measure?

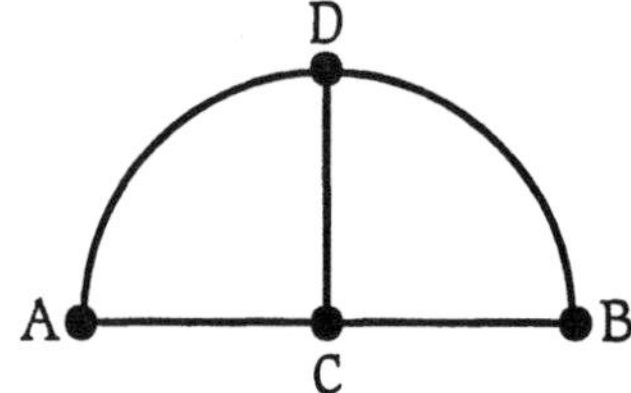

Fold your half–circle into sixths, as shown. Using a straight edge and a pencil, trace the fold lines. Label these four new fold lines EC, FC, GC, and HC.

- What do you think angle ACE measures? Verify your answer with your teacher.

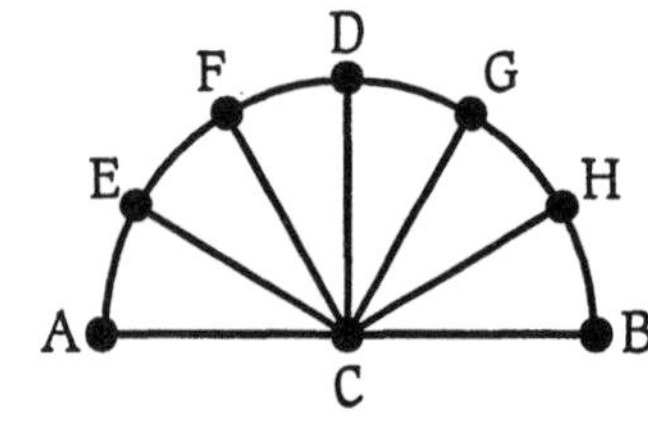

Tape your protractor to a piece of paper. Label your protractor. Beginning with angle ACE, label all lines. Some of the lines have been labeled in the example to help you.

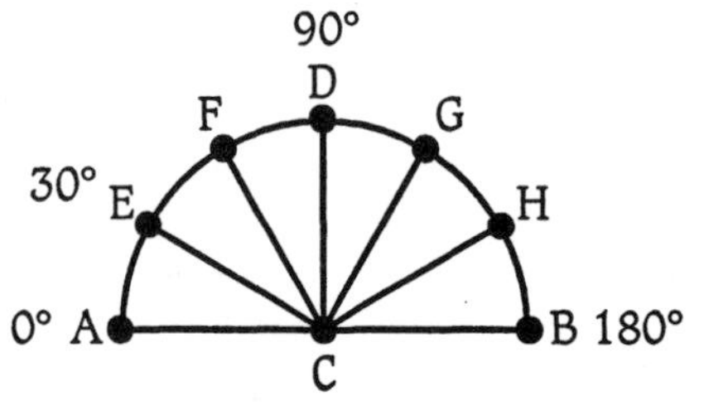

Geometry Readiness

POINTS, LINES, AND ANGLES

Study the figure below.

Classify the following angles as either acute, right, obtuse, or straight. Using the diagram, determine the measure of each angle.

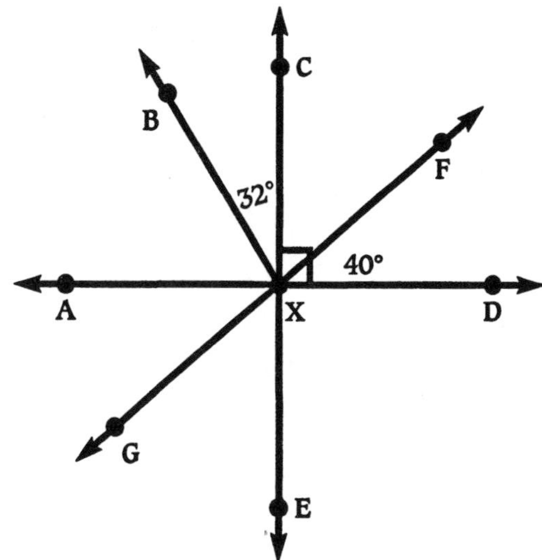

	Angle	Type	Measure
1.	∠ AXB	acute	58°
2.	∠ CXE	________	________
3.	∠ CXF	________	________
4.	∠ DXE	________	________
5.	∠ EXG	________	________
6.	∠ GXA	________	________
7.	∠ GXB	________	________
8.	∠ BXF	________	________
9.	∠ CXD	________	________
10.	∠ FXE	________	________
11.	∠ AXD	________	________
12.	∠ EXA	________	________

Geometry Readiness

Name ______________________________ Date ____________

Geometry Flash Cards

Make each student a set of geometry flash cards to allow them to practice identifying specific types of angles or reading the correct angle measurement. On the back of each flash card, classify each angle as either acute, right, obtuse, or straight and write the measurement of each angle.

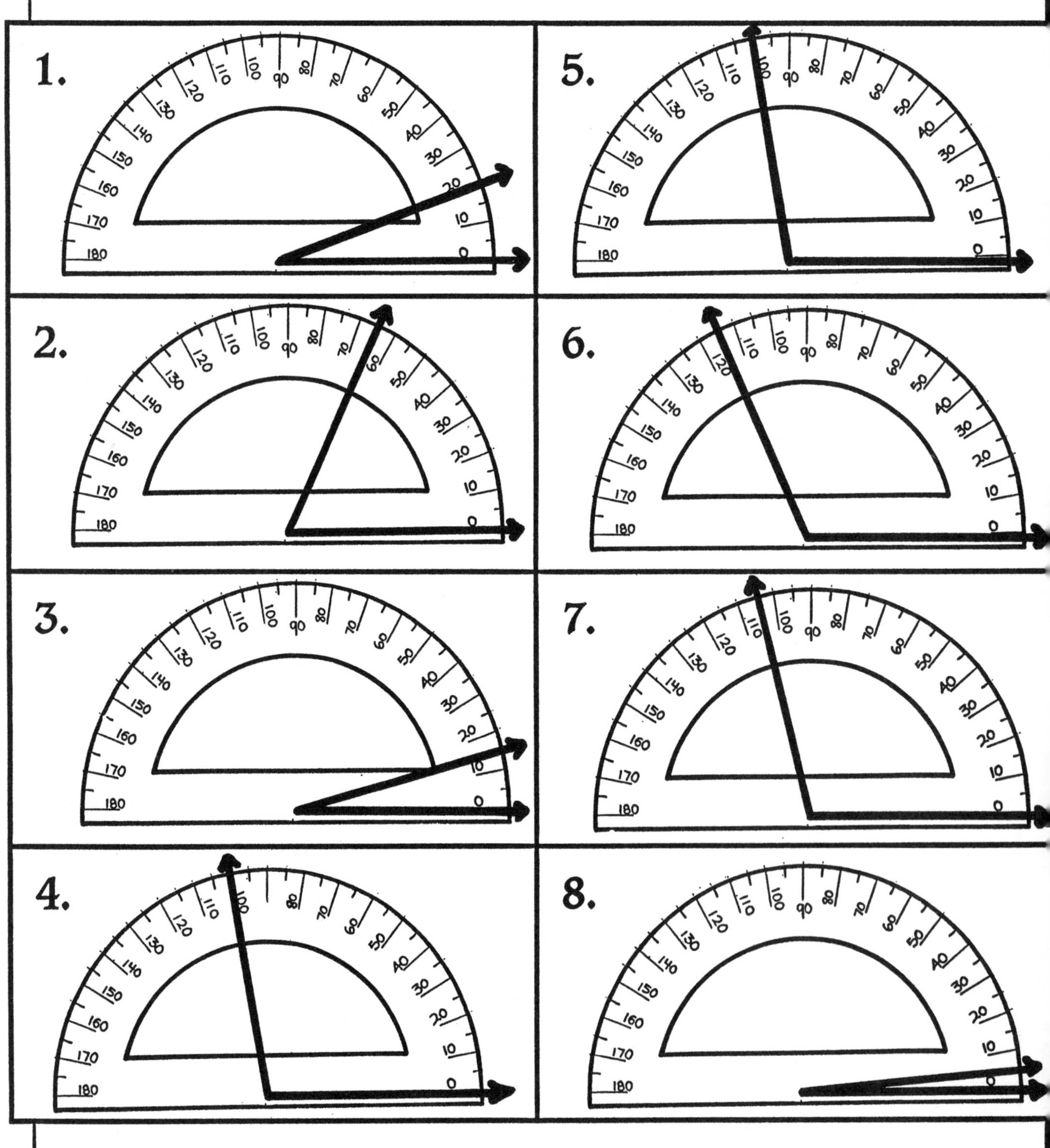

Geometry Flash Cards

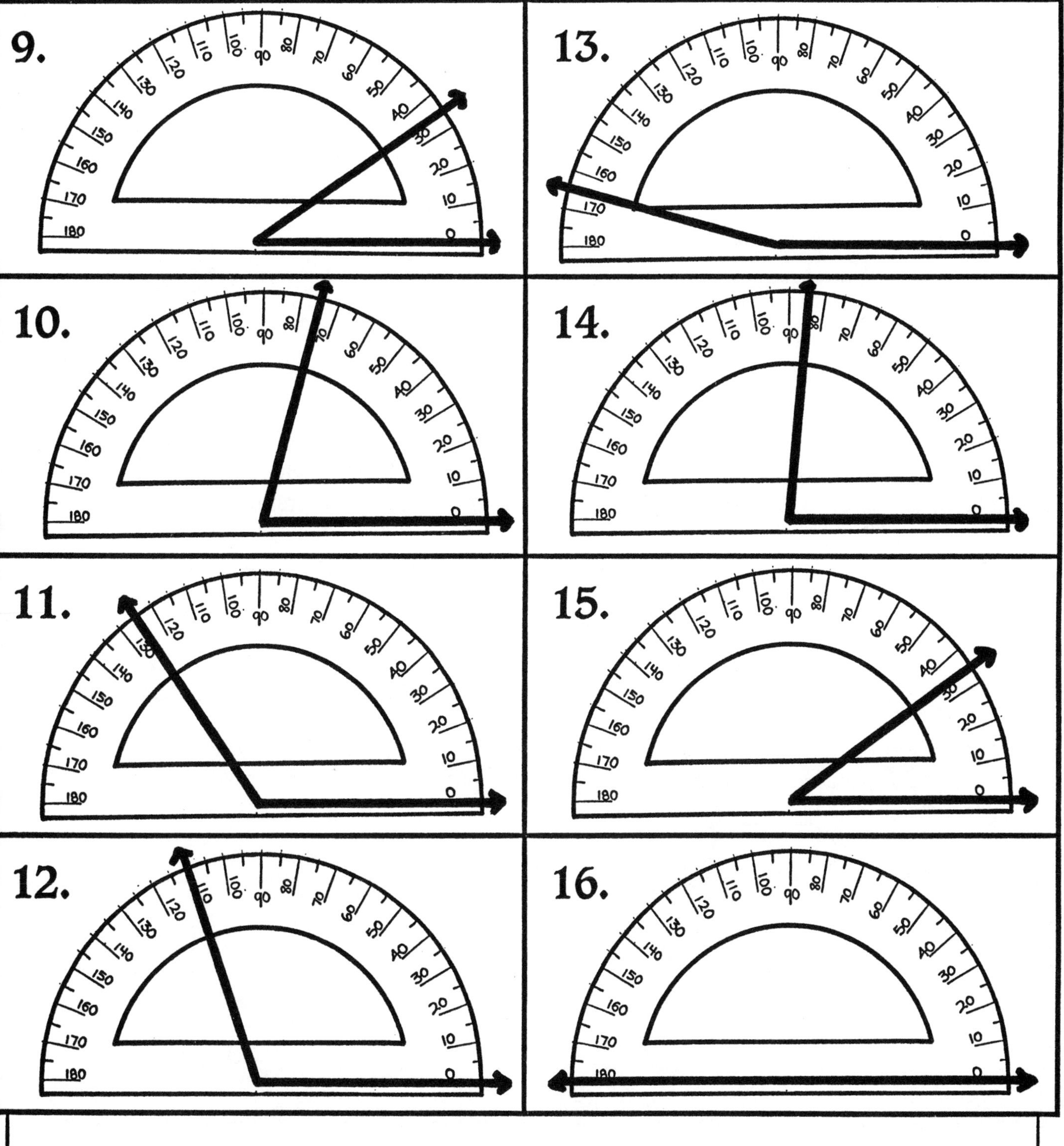

Puzzling Perimeters

Pete was puzzled. He proposed perimeter problems to his peers. Perhaps you can predict the perimeters or lengths of the sides of these polygons.

Puzzler 1

This pentagon has a perimeter of 50m. Propose the only possible length for Side P.

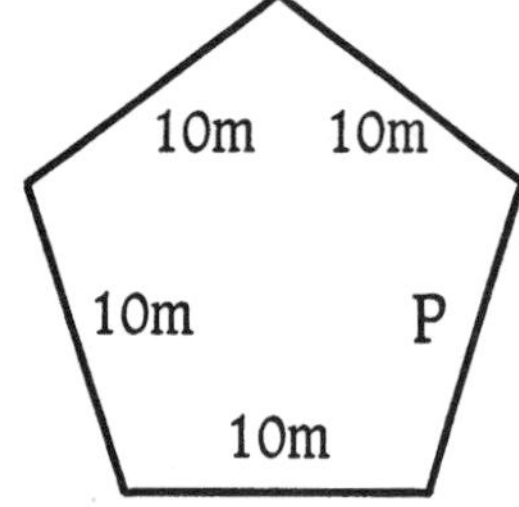

Puzzler 2

This particular polygon was preying on the pupils' minds. Preview it and predict the perfect length for Side P.

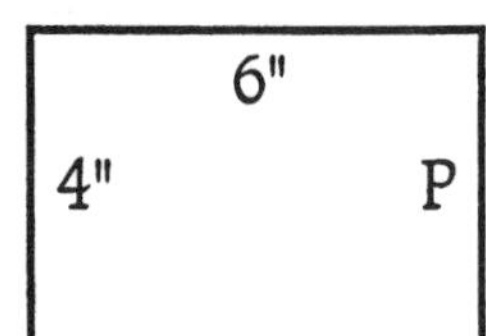

Puzzler 3

It was presumed that this proper polygon (a square) has the perimeter of 16cm. Perhaps you can write a paragraph explaining why this is a good premise.

Puzzler 4

Please don't panic! This polygon is perhaps less of a pain than you presumed. It's a regular polygon. With patience and the particular partial data, you can predict its perimeter.

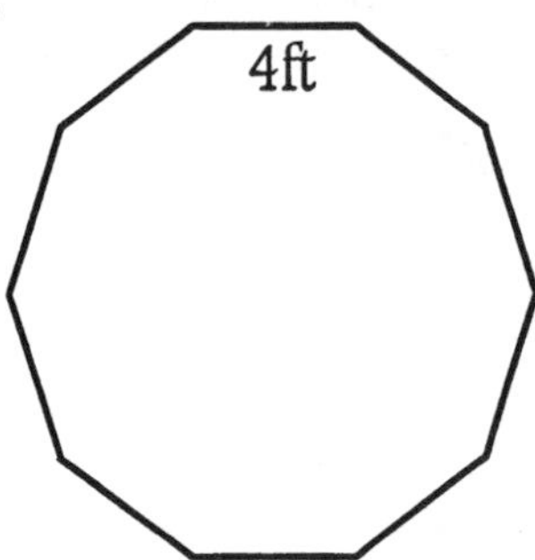

Geometry Readiness

Name ______________________________ Date ______________

LET ME DRAW YOU A PICTURE!

Finding area can be fun and can be an avenue for displaying your creativity. There is an old saying, "There is more than one way to skin a cat." Well, there are other ways to find the area of a surface besides memorizing all of the different formulas for area. This activity requires imagination and cooperation. Let's see if you can picture this.

Group Size:

Two

Materials Needed:

- Dot paper (see page 117 for pattern, or supply your own)
- Pencil

Procedure:

1. Using two sheets of dot paper, each student creates two versions of an original geometric design.
2. The first copy is to be sectioned off in squares or triangles to determine the area.
3. The second copy is to be used to apply Pic's Formula.
4. Each student is to name the design created. The students exchange designs with their partners and determine the area of the designs.
5. The teams compare their answers. If the team members disagree on a particular response, they should work together to determine the correct area of the design using sectional squares and triangles or Pic's Formula.

The area enclosed within your design may be found by using PIC'S FORMULA:

AREA = ($\frac{1}{2}$ border dots) + interior dots – 1

Border Dots – the dots touching the design

Interior Dots – the dots inside of the design

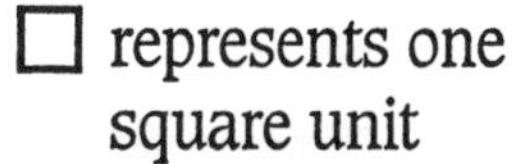

□ represents one square unit

◺ represents one–half square unit

Example: 52 Border Dots
49 Interior Dots

Area = ($\frac{1}{2}$ x 52) + 49 – 1
= 26 + 49 – 1
= 74

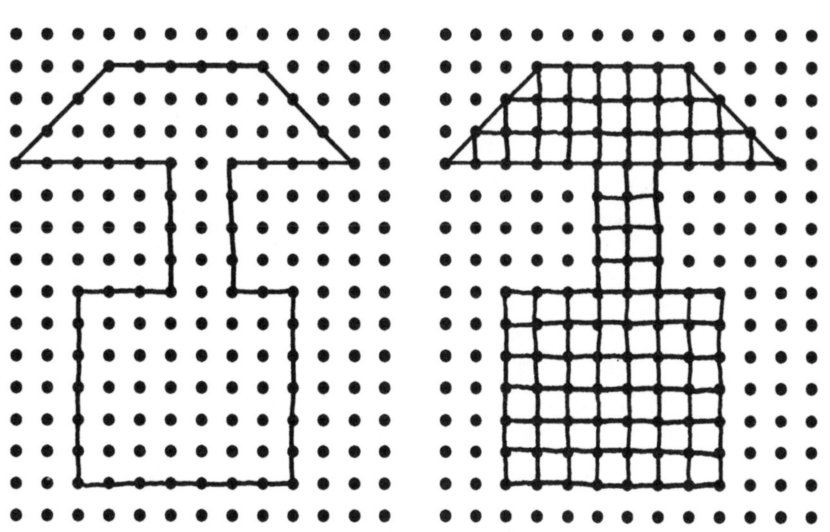

Geometry Readiness

Polygon Nim

As legend goes, nim games originated in China. The term nim means "to pilfer." Read the directions below to determine how to swipe your partner's pattern blocks.

To Play:

The polygon pattern on page 103 was created using the following pattern block pieces: 4 large rhombi, 8 triangles, 6 hexagons, 4 small rhombi, 4 squares, and 4 trapezoids. Create a pattern block bank using these same pieces. (Reproducible patterns are on page 118.)

Spread out the polygon pieces so that Player 1 (you) and Player 2 can easily reach them. Player 1 can decide if he or she wants to select one, two, or three pattern pieces from the bank. (All pieces selected must be different polygons.) Player 1 places the selected pieces on the polygon pattern.

Player 2 now decides if he or she wants to select and play one, two, or three pieces from the bank. Remember, the pieces must all be different polygons, and all pieces must be played.

A player can play a piece, such as a triangle, as a fractional portion of another polygon. The piece must not be placed across solid lines, and it must be a legitimate fit within the polygon.

Play continues with each player selecting polygons and laying the pieces on the pattern. Remember, a piece laid is a piece played. The game ends when one player has been able to play a final piece. This player is the winner. A winner can also be determined if one player has selected a polygon that cannot be played on the board. This player automatically loses the game.

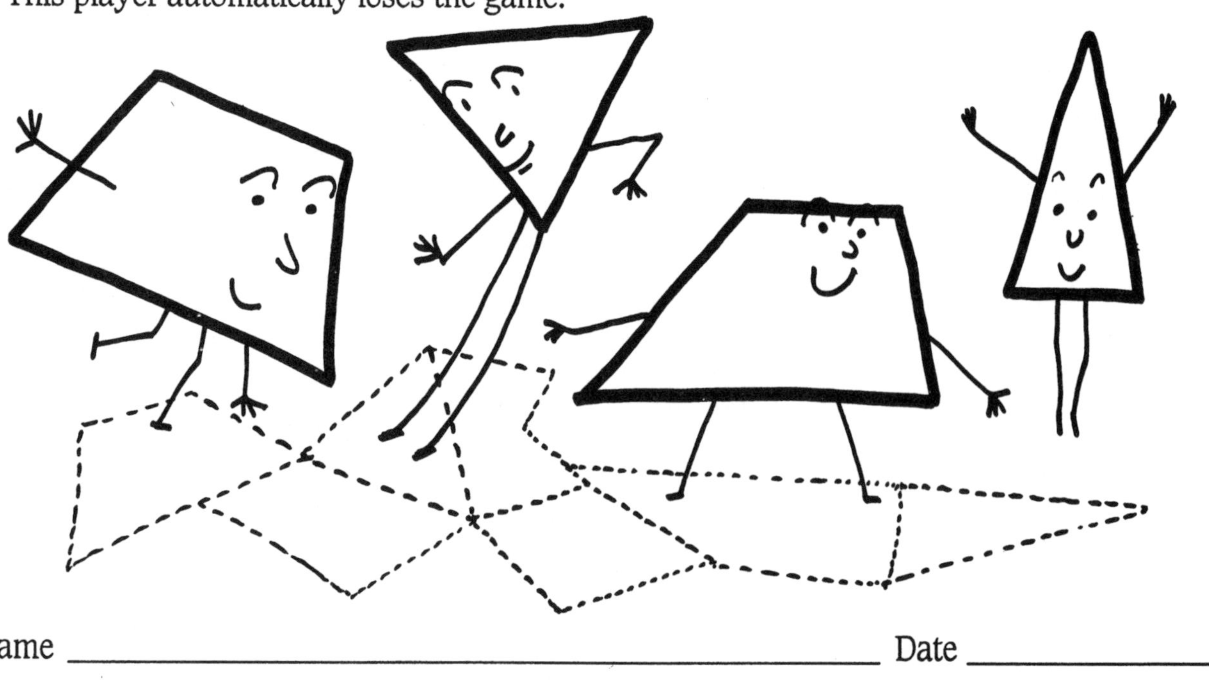

Geometry Readiness

Name ______________________________ Date ____________

Polygon Patterns

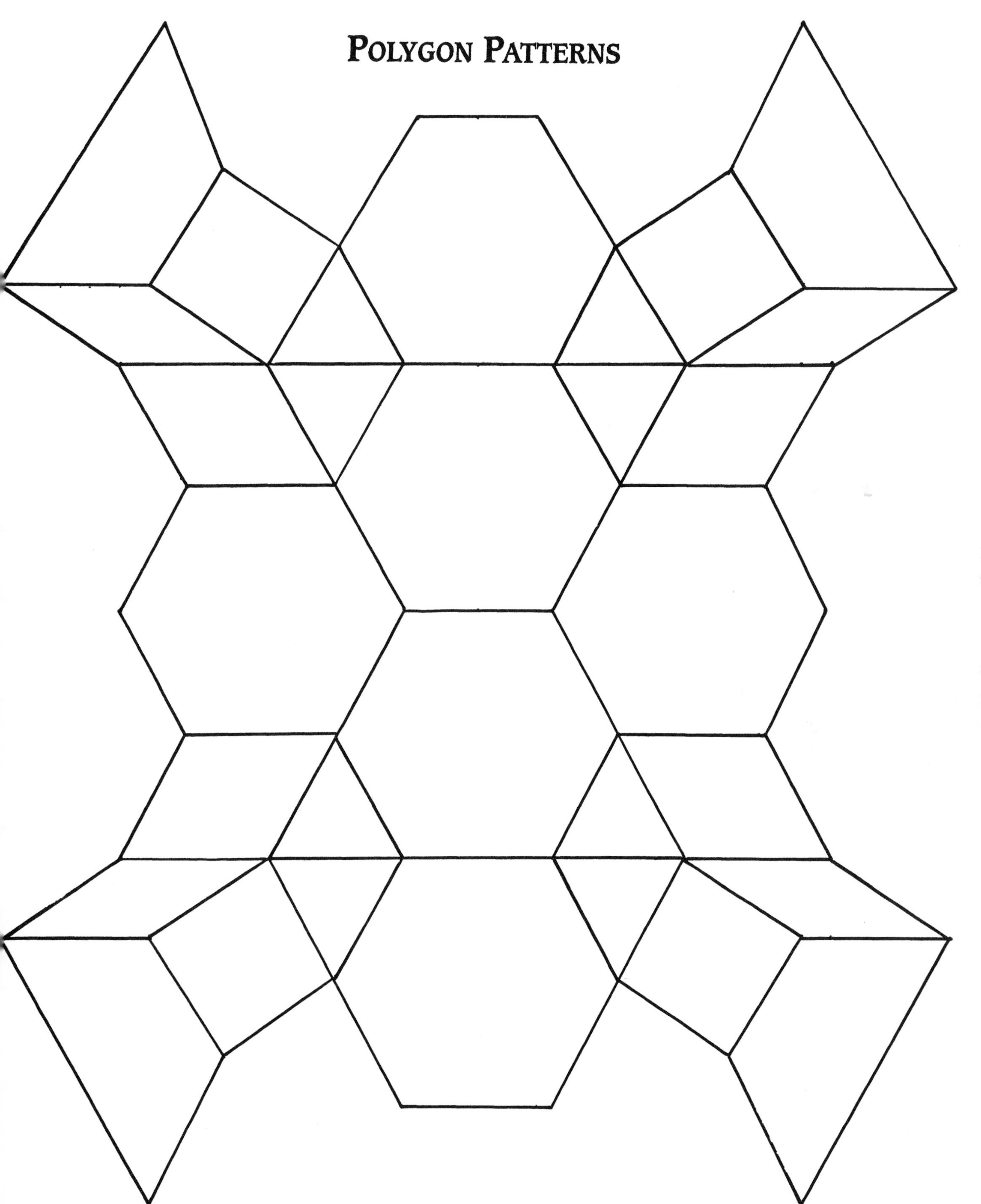

ARE YOU IN A QUANDARY ABOUT QUADRILATERALS?

Quadrilaterals are figures with four sides. That's it . . . it's simple! The confusion may come when you hear the words rectangle, square, trapezoid, or rhombus. Review the definitions below, then practice what you have learned by correctly coloring the geometric design below.

- Rectangle: A quadrilateral with four right angles and with opposite sides that are parallel.
- Square: A quadrilateral with four right angles and four equal sides.
- Trapezoid: A quadrilateral with exactly one pair of opposite sides that are parallel.
- Rhombus: A quadrilateral with four congruent sides and with opposite sides that are parallel.

Coloring Chart

Color each quadrilateral according to this chart.

- Rectangle = red
- Rhombus = black
- Square = blue
- Trapezoid = green
- None of these quadrilaterals, but a four-sided polygon = purple

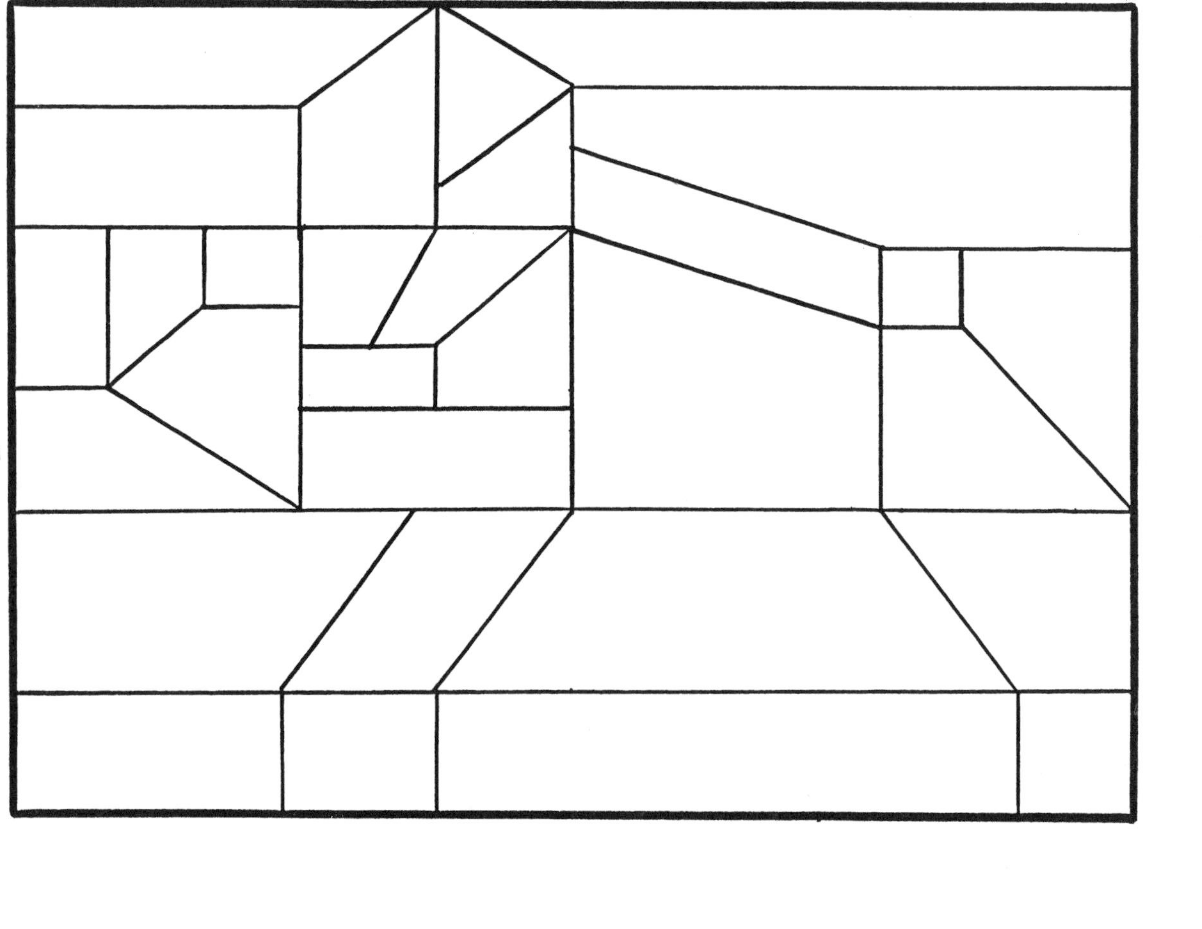

Name ______________________ Date ____________

Triangle Scramble

Cut out the polygons in each scramble and use the shapes to create a triangle

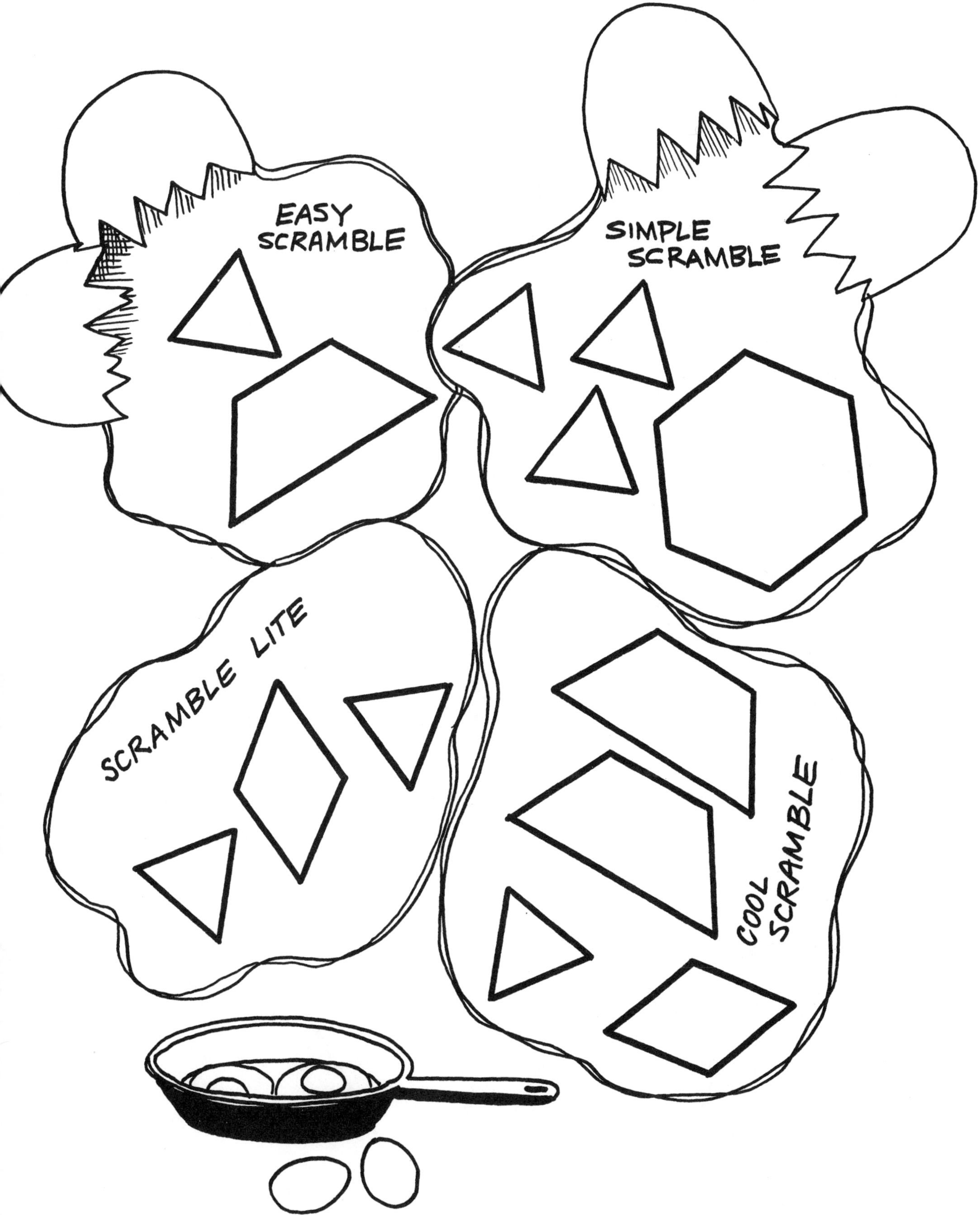

Spatial Visualization

TRIANGLE SCRAMBLE

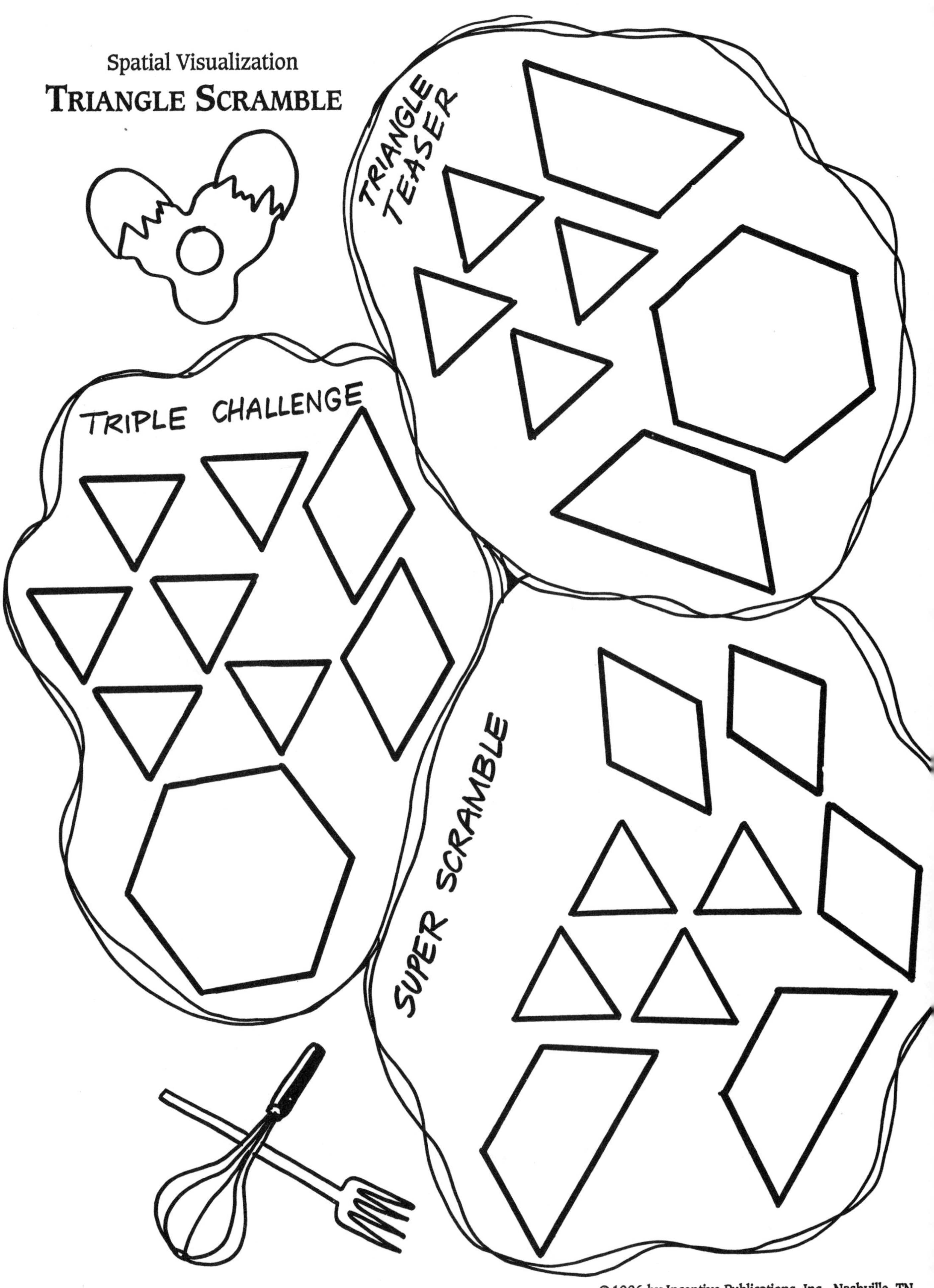

Geometry Logic

Player 1 prepares a 3 x 3 grid (pattern, page 109), using three geometric shapes. Each geometric shape must be connected by at least one full side.

For example, a secret grid might look like this:

	Column A	Column B	Column C
Row 3	Square	Hexagon	Hexagon
Row 2	Square	Square	Hexagon
Row 1	Rhombus	Rhombus	Rhombus

Clues are given when Player 2 asks questions to Player 1 in the following manner: "What polygons are in Row 3?" The polygons are then named in any order (answer: "Hexagon, Square, Hexagon"). Polygon pieces may be placed beside the rows or columns until the exact place is determined. "What polygons are in Column C?" (answer: "Rhombus, Hexagon, Hexagon"). At this point, Player 2 should attempt to place the polygons on the 3 x 3 grid. Placing the pieces will help the player keep track of the clues. Play is continued until Player 2 has replicated Player 1's design.

The following patterns are not allowed because the sides are not adjacent.

	Column A	Column B	Column C
Row 3	Square		
Row 2		Square	
Row 1			Square

	Column A	Column B	Column C
Row 3		Square	
Row 2			Square
Row 1		Square	

A 4 x 4 grid is provided for more advanced players (page 109). Use a triangle as the fourth polygon for this grid formation.

Pattern pieces are on page 108.

Name ______________________________ Date ______________

Geometry Readiness

GEOMETRY LOGIC

Patterns:

- For a game on a 3 x 3 grid, each player should receive 3 hexagons, 3 rhombi, and 3 squares.
- For a game on a 4 x 4 grid, each player should receive 4 hexagons, 4 rhombi, 4 squares, and 4 triangles.

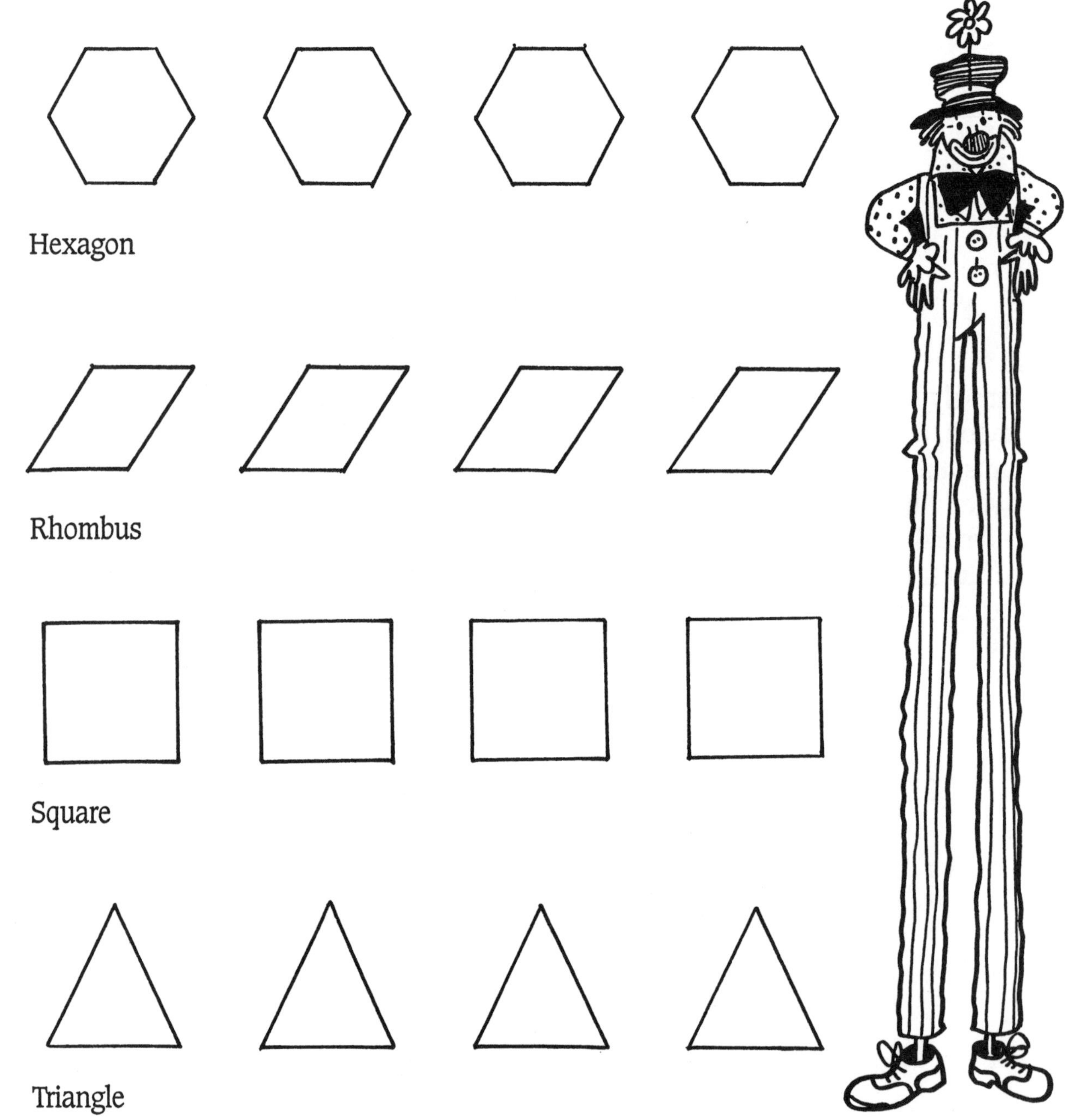

Geometry Logic

3 x 3 Grid

	Column A	Column B	Column C
Row 3			
Row 2			
Row 1			

4 x 4 Grid

	Column A	Column B	Column C	Column D
Row 4				
Row 3				
Row 2				
Row 1				

Symmetry And More!

Step 1 On the line below each polygon, write the name of the shape (triangle, quadrilateral, pentagon, hexagon, octagon, or decagon).

Step 2 Draw all possible lines of symmetry on each of the polygons.

Step 3 Using the chart at the bottom of the page, list the polygons which contain specific lines of symmetry.

Example:

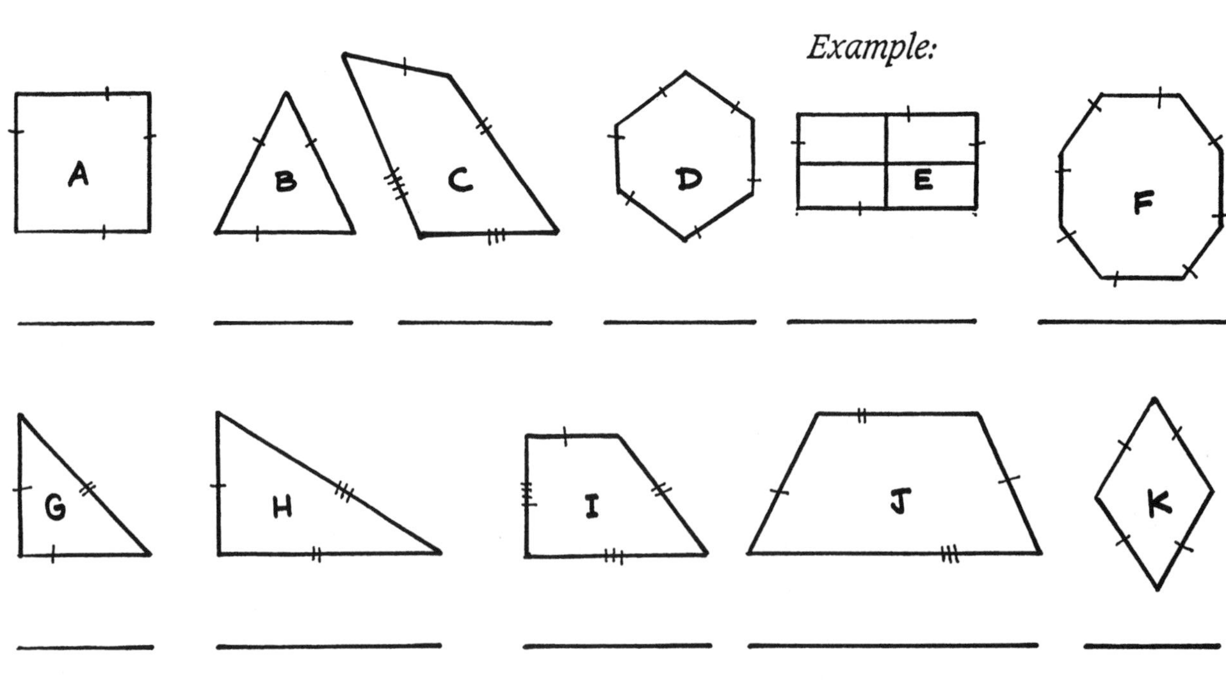

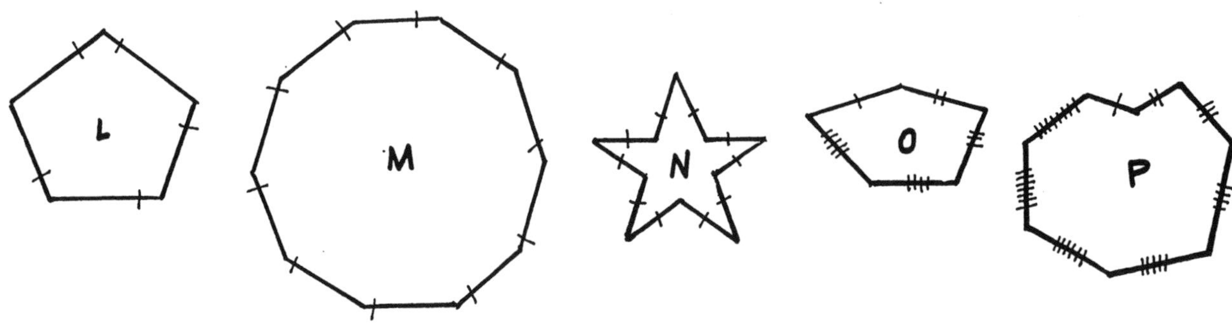

Line(s) of Symmetry

Which figures contain . . .

. . . no lines of symmetry ____________

. . . one line of symmetry ____________

. . . two lines of symmetry E, ____________

. . . three lines of symmetry ____________

. . . four or more lines of symmetry ____________

Name ______________________ Date ____________

Geometry Readiness

An Introduction To Tessellations: T Is For Tessellations!

The letter T is just one of the letters of the alphabet that will tessellate. The word tessellation is used when referring to shapes that when placed side by side do not have any gaps or do not overlap with one another.

Start with the letter T shown on the dot paper below. Fill the dot paper with Ts so that there are no overlaps or gaps on the paper. If you prefer, make several cardboard templates of the T to assist you. When the entire paper is filled, color the design so that no T touches another T of the same color. Use the least possible number of colors.

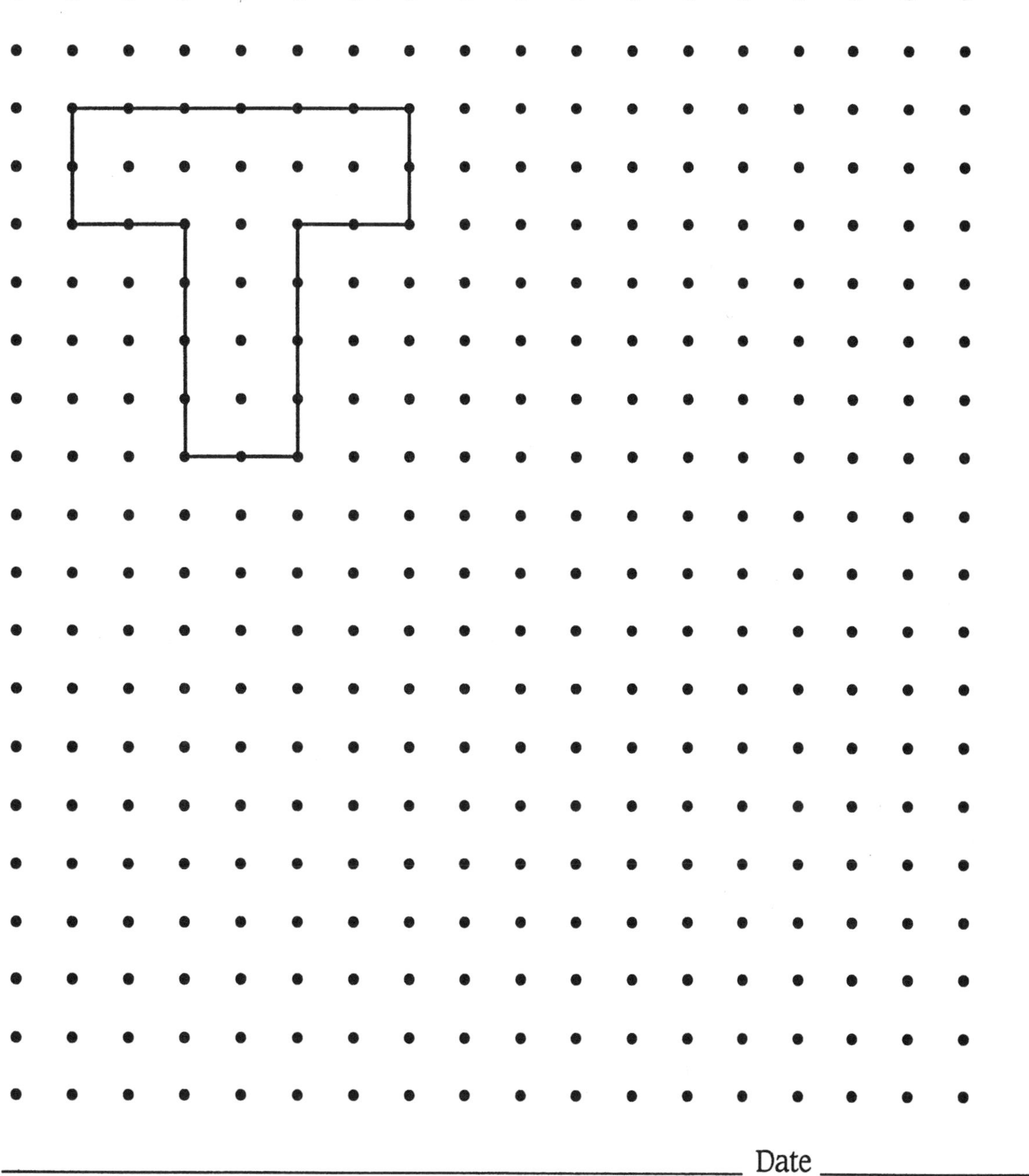

Name ______________________________ Date ______________

Geometry Readiness

TESSELLATION COMBINATION

Polygons will tessellate around a vertex point if the sum of their interior angles equals 360°. Measure and label all interior angles of the polygons on page 113. After all interior angles are determined, you will be ready to play Tessellation Combination.

To Play:

1. Each group (either two students or two teams) should cut out and assemble a Combination Tessellation Spinner (pattern below).
2. Player 1 spins the spinner and notes the polygon that spinner lands on. Player 1 spins again and notes the second polygon that the spinner lands on.
3. Player 1 uses the information from page 113 to determine if those two polygons can tessellate. The player has the option of adding additional polygons to form a tessellation, but they must be the same types of polygons as were originally spun. For example, if the two polygons that a player landed on were an equilateral triangle and a regular hexagon, a tessellation could be formed using two hexagons (120° + 120° = 240°) and two equilateral triangles (60° + 60° = 120°). All interior angles total 360°.
4. Player 1 states if a tessellation can or cannot be formed. If Player 2 agrees, Player 1 receives 10 points. If Player 2 disagrees, Player 1 must draw a diagram of the tessellation to prove the answer. If Player 1 is wrong, he or she loses 5 points. If Player 2 is wrong, he or she loses 5 points.
5. The spinner is passed to Player 2 and the game continues in the same fashion. The player with the most points after ten spins wins the game.

Combination Tessellation Spinner

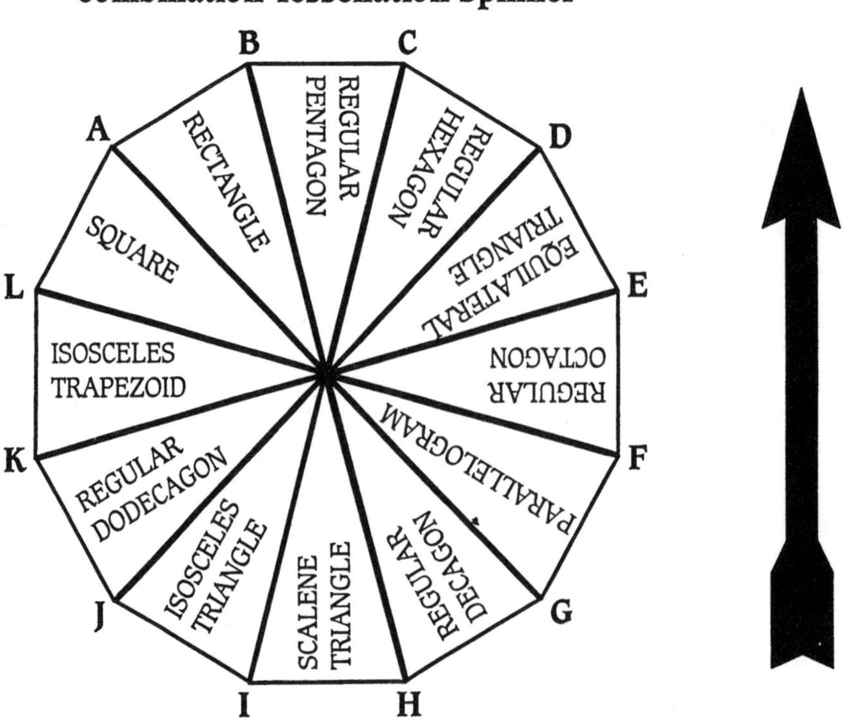

Geometry Readiness

TESSELLATION COMBINATIONS

Measure all interior angles.

Rectangle

Regular Pentagon

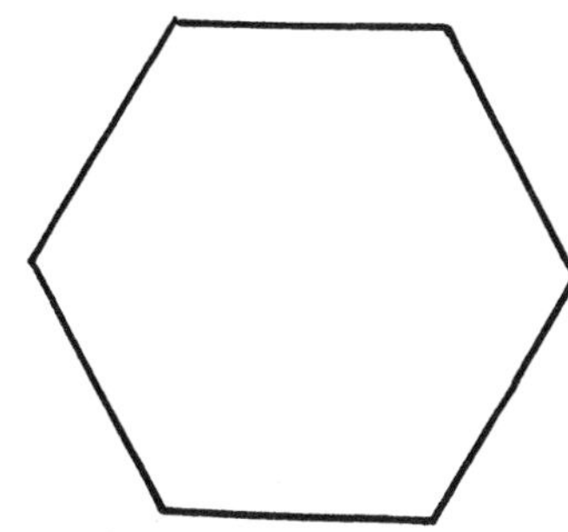

Regular Hexagon

Equilateral Triangle

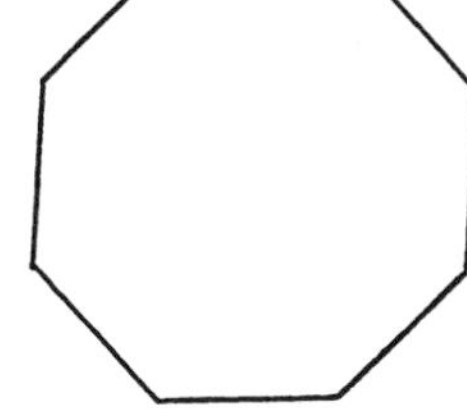

Regular Octagon

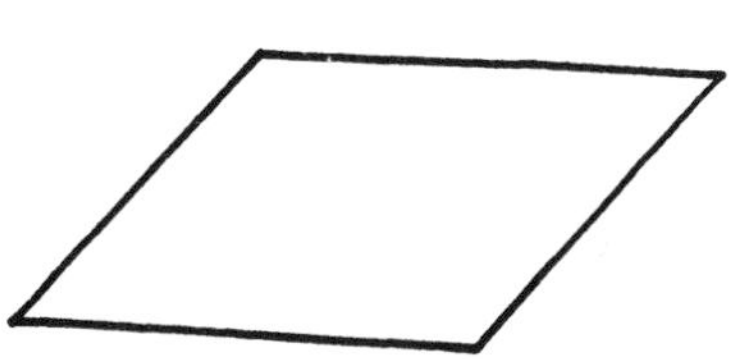

Parallelogram

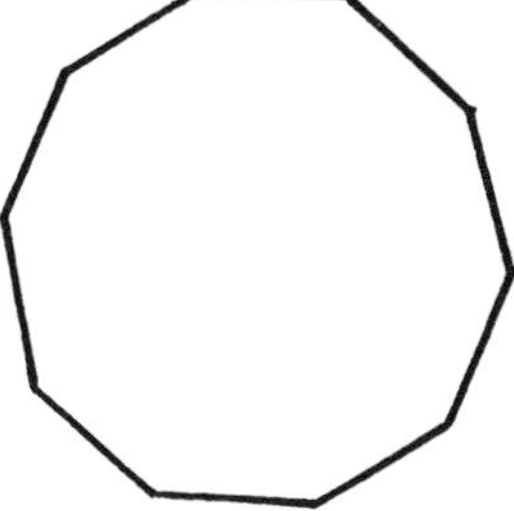

Regular Decagon

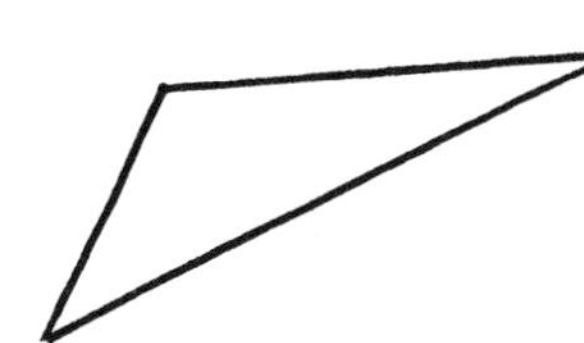

Scalene Triangle

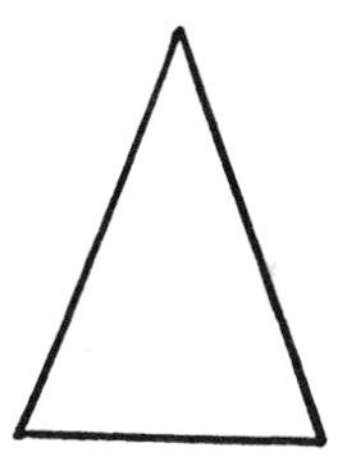

Iscoceles Triangle

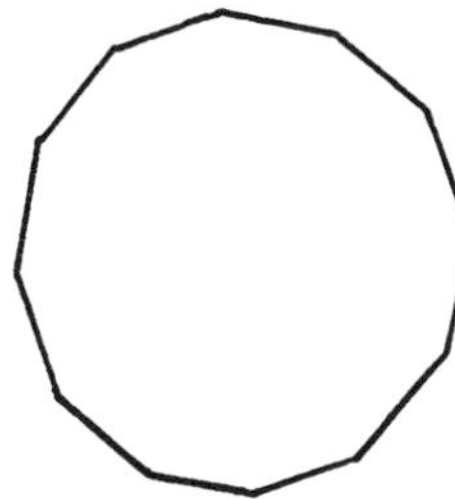

Regular Dodecagon

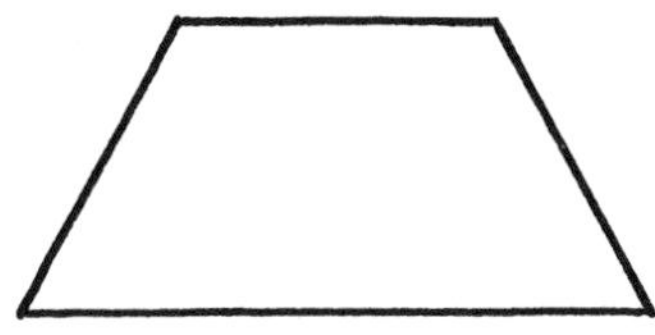

Isosceles Trapezoid

Square

Double–check your measurements of all of the regular polygons.

Using the formula $(n-2)180/n$ you can determine if your angle measurements of the regular polygons are accurate. (The variable n is equal to the number of sides of the regular polygons.)

An Example Of Similarity

In mathematics, a fractal is any shape or process that can be described as having self-symmetry (in other words, if any portion of the shape is a reduced copy of either the entire shape or some larger portion of the shape). The similarity continues with the parts of the parts of the shape to infinity. This process of repetition is sometimes called iteration.

Broccoli and cauliflower are two simple examples of fractals observed in the natural world. Ferns, mountain ranges, trees, and seashells are others.

In the example below, a line is divided into three parts and the middle part is removed.

Step 1: Line segment

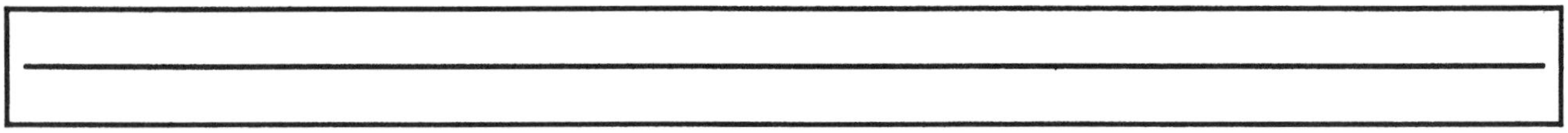

Step 2: Divide into 3 parts

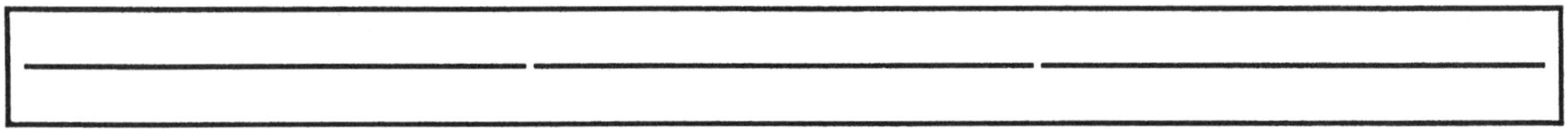

Step 3: Remove middle part

This process is repeated again and again with the two remaining parts until there are an infinite number of parts which are too small to be seen.

Step 4

Step 5

Step 6

Step 7

Step 8

Step 9

Step 10

Step 11

Step 12

The line segments have now become too small to be seen. However, this process repeats infinitely, with the number of line segments increasing and each line length decreasing. Notice that each segment, no matter how small, is similar in scale to the original line segment.

Resources and References

DOT PAPER

PATTERN BLOCKS

SCORE CARD

ROUND	PLAYER	PLAYER	PLAYER	PLAYER
1				
2				
3				
4				
5				
6				
7				
8				
9				
10				

ROUND	PLAYER	PLAYER	PLAYER	PLAYER
1				
2				
3				
4				
5				
6				
7				
8				
9				
10				

ROUND	PLAYER	PLAYER	PLAYER	PLAYER
1				
2				
3				
4				
5				
6				
7				
8				
9				
10				

Answer Keys

Page 9

18	[illegible]	16	14	26	48	24	88	46	72	92
[illegible]	2	[illegible]	28	30	98	[illegible]	50	86	90	[illegible]
[illegible]	20	[illegible]	4	24	52	[illegible]	20	10	66	[illegible]
[illegible]	32	[illegible]	40	6	100	[illegible]	54	30	56	[illegible]
[illegible]	22	[illegible]	12	[illegible]	[illegible]	[illegible]	44	[illegible]	[illegible]	[illegible]
[illegible]	34	[illegible]	42	[illegible]	8	[illegible]	60	[illegible]	58	[illegible]
[illegible]	38	[illegible]	10	[illegible]	62	[illegible]	402	[illegible]	60	[illegible]
36	[illegible]	46	44	[illegible]	[illegible]	[illegible]	40	[illegible]	[illegible]	[illegible]

Page 17

Set One	Set Two	Set Three
(6, 6)	(–8, –5)	(7, –2)
(9, 2)	(–5, –2)	(4, –2)
(6, 2)	(–7, –7)	(–5, 1)
(15, 1)	(–6, –2)	(3, –2)
(9, 4)	(–5, –1)	(–8, 5)
(3, 2)	(–2, –1)	(–5, 2)
(8, 1)	(–3, –2)	(8, –3)
(9, 1)	(–1, –1)	(–8, 2)
(6, 3)	(–7, –2)	(8, –7)
(4, 3)	(–7, –4)	(–6, 2)
(5, 3)	(–4, –3)	(11, –3)
(6, 1)	(–5, –6)	(–8, 3)
(3, 3)	(–11, –3)	(8, –2)
(18, 1)	(–9, –3)	(–9, 7)
(4, 2)	(–8, –3)	(5, –3)
(8, 5)	(–10, –1)	(6, –5)
(12, 1)	(–6, –3)	(5, –4)
(5, 4)	(–2, –2)	(7, –5)
(7, 3)	(–6, –4)	(–6, 4)
(8, 3)	(–5, –4)	(–8, 4)
(10, 3)	(–8, –2)	(–6, 2)
(7, 2)	(–5, –3)	(–3, 2)
(6, 4)	(–9, –2)	(–7, 1)
(6, 7)	(–3, –3)	(7, –3)
(10, 2)	(–15, –1)	(7, –1)
(9, 3)	(–7, –1)	(–5, 3)
(21, 3)	(–9, –1)	(7, –4)
(22, 2)	(–13, –1)	(8, –4)
(12, 6)	(–23, –1)	(14, –2)
(23, 1)	(–17, –3)	(16, –4)
(25, 3)	(–19, –3)	
(7, 5)	(–29, –1)	

Page 19

1. $\frac{12 \bullet 15}{3}$, LCM = 60
2. $\frac{16 \bullet 88}{8}$, LCM = 176
3. $\frac{12 \bullet 35}{1}$, LCM = 420
4. $\frac{20 \bullet 50}{10}$, LCM = 100
5. $\frac{12 \bullet 8}{4}$, LCM = 24
6. $\frac{21 \bullet 14}{7}$, LCM = 42
7. $\frac{13 \bullet 39}{13}$, LCM = 39
8. $\frac{7 \bullet 13}{1}$, LCM = 91
9. $\frac{28 \bullet 42}{14}$, LCM = 84
10. $\frac{5 \bullet 6}{1}$, LCM = 30

Page 20

1. $\frac{43}{40}$ or $1\frac{3}{40}$
2. $\frac{60}{63}$
3. $\frac{83}{110}$
4. $\frac{272}{45}$ or $6\frac{2}{45}$
5. $\frac{199}{18}$ or $11\frac{1}{18}$
6. $\frac{9}{8}$ or $1\frac{1}{8}$
7. $\frac{267}{20}$ or $13\frac{7}{20}$
8. $\frac{129}{119}$ or $1\frac{10}{119}$
9. $\frac{127}{18}$ or $7\frac{1}{18}$
10. $\frac{29}{18}$ or $1\frac{11}{18}$
11. $\frac{1637}{1071}$ or $1\frac{566}{1071}$
12. $\frac{41}{36}$ or $1\frac{5}{36}$
13. $\frac{5}{6}$
14. $\frac{37}{30}$ or $1\frac{7}{30}$
15. $\frac{121}{90}$ or $1\frac{31}{90}$

Page 23

1. False
2. True
3. False
4. True
5. True
6. True
7. False

Page 24

1. one
2. equal
3. onetenth
3. onefourth
4. twenty
5. aquarter
6. reciprocal
7. nine
8. two
9. third
9. ten
10. one
11. ten
12. zero
13. six
14. mixednumeral

Page 26

Set One:	(12, 24)
Set Two:	(0, 1)
Set Three:	(7, 11)
Set Four:	(98, 100)
Set Five:	(8, 64)
Set Six:	(10, 5)

Page 27

1. $x = 9.8$
2. $x = 13.3$
3. $w = 0.42$
4. $s = 6.4$
5. $p = 3.56$
6. $t = 2.89$
7. $h = 16.3$
8. $y = 21.7$
9. $p = 3.9$
10. $b = 1.6$
11. $u = 3.77$
12. $k = 7.5$
13. $d = 3.38$
14. $g = 25.2$
15. $x = 14.7$
16. $x = 0.9$
17. $g = 17.3$
18. $j = 20.58$
19. $g = 3.5$
20. $h = 80.78$
21. $f = 92.06$
22. $d = 38.1$
23. $g = 17.8$
24. $r = 13.8$
25. $k = 0.08$

Page 29

A = 26⁄100 (26 hundredths)
.26
26 percent

E = 23⁄100 (23 hundredths)
.23
23 percent

I = 28⁄100 (28 hundredths)
.28
28 percent

O = 28⁄100 (28 hundredths)
.28
28 percent

U = 24⁄100 (24 hundredths)
.24
24 percent

Page 35

Mary Smart

1. 1000
2. 1000
3. 1840
4. 1840
5. 2775
6. 2775
7. 3990
8. 3990

Mary applied the commutative property of addition to the odd-numbered problems.

Q. W. Quincy

1. 582
2. 157
3. 82
4. $24.00
5. $36.00
6. 247
7. 334

Quincy applied the associative property to each problem.

Pages 39-40 (Suggested answers are provided. Answers may vary.)

Set One: The third number is the sum of the first and second numbers. (1 + 2 = 3)
Set Two: The first number is the sum of the second and third numbers. (4 + 2 = 6)
Set Three: The first number is the product of the second and third numbers. (4 x 7 = 28)
Set Four: The third number is one more than the sum of the first and second numbers. ([2 + 4] + 1 = 7)
Set Five: The third number is one less than the difference between the first and second numbers. ([8 – 3] – 1 = 4)
Set Six: The third number is the product of the second number and the difference between the second and first numbers. ([4 – 2] x 4 = 8)

Page 43

$5 + x =$ a. 2 b. 22 c. -2	$(x + 5) \div 2 =$ a. 8 b. 50 c. 2.5 or $2\frac{1}{2}$	$2^x =$ a. 8 b. 32 c. 1	$(-5)^x =$ a. -125 b. 25 c. -5
$(24 \div x) - 1 =$ a. 5 b. 1 c. -13	$x^3 =$ a. 27 b. 125 c. -1	$6x^2 =$ a. 54 b. 6 c. 0	$-5^x =$ a. -125 b. -25 c. -5
$2(x - 19) =$ a. 162 b. 36 c. -76	$40 \div x =$ a. 8 b. -2 c. $\frac{2}{3}$	$x^2 + 4x + 4 =$ a. 25 b. 49 c. 4	$(-x)^4 =$ a. 16 b. 1 c. 0
$9x =$ a. 36 b. 117 c. -54	$(x + 7) \div 3 =$ a. 4 b. 20 c. $2\frac{1}{3}$	$(x + 1)^2 =$ a. 49 b. 25 c. 4	$(-4)^x =$ a. -64 b. 16 c. -4
$x + 7 =$ a. 5 b. 100 c. -7	$x^4 =$ a. 16 b. 81 c. 1	$(3x)^2 =$ a. 9 b. 36 c. 0	$-4^x =$ a. -64 b. -16 c. -4
$(72 \div x) + 5 =$ a. 17 b. 13 c. -4	$3^x =$ a. 9 b. 81 c. 3	$56 - 6x =$ a. 8 b. 50 c. 56	$-x =$ a. -5 b. 3 c. 1
$4(x - 31) =$ a. 196 b. 104 c. -84	$4x^2 =$ a. 36 b. 0 c. 100	$(x + 2)^2 =$ a. 25 b. 49 c. 4	$(-1)(x) =$ a. -5 b. 3 c. 1
$7x =$ a. 56 b. 77 c. -42	$x^2 + 2x + 1 =$ a. 49 b. 25 c. 4	$(5x)^2 =$ a. 25 b. 100 c. 0	$15 \div x =$ a. 3 b. -5 c. -15
$30 \div x =$ a. 5 b. $-\frac{1}{3}$ c. $\frac{2}{3}$	$(-x)^2 =$ a. 9 b. 1 c. 4	$108 - 8x =$ a. 12 b. 100 c. 108	$x + 3 =$ a. -2 b. 6 c. 3

Page 45

1. $8x - 3y$ (E)
2. $12a + 6$ (D)
3. y (M)
4. $-y$ (M)
5. $17b - c$ (T)
6. $14y - x$ (I)
7. a (L)
8. $7x + 3y$ (T)
9. $6a + 1$ (N)
10. $-16x - 3$ (K)
11. -3 (E)
12. $8x - 3$ (M)
13. $3b^2 + 9b$ (E)
14. $8x^2 + 2x$ (T)
15. $5a + 1$ (S)
16. $3ab + 2a$ (E)
17. $20xy + 12y$ (C)
18. $9x^2y + 3xy^2$ (V)
19. $10ab - 3$ (H)
20. $-9x + 1$ (C)
21. $5x^2 + 11$ (Y)
22. $4b + 4$ (I)
23. $2y^2 + 3y$ (A)
24. $4x^2 + 4$ (A)
25. $-a + 6b + 2$ (O)

Detective Mathlock is my name.

Pages 55–56

A = Commutative Property of Addition
B = Commutative Property of Addition
C = Inverse Property of Multiplication
D = Closure Property of Addition
E = Commutative Property of Multiplication
F = Inverse Property of Addition
G = Closure Property of Multiplication
H = No, because a number multiplied by zero equals zero, not the original value of the number.
I = Associative Property of Addition
J = Identity Element of Multiplication
K = Inverse Property of Addition
L = No, because one does not give the original value of the number. It only *increases* the value by one.
M = Identity Element of Addition
N = Identity Element of Addition
O = Inverse Property of Multiplication
P = No, a property is a statement that is true for every real number.
Q = Identity Element of Multiplication
R = Commutative Property of Addition
S = Transitive property
T = 0 (Zero)
U = Commutative Property of Multiplication
V = Associative Property of Multiplication
W = Transitive Property
X = $-5 + 5$
Y = Associative Property of Multiplication
Z = Associative Property of Addition
AA = Symmetric Property
BB = Identity Element of Multiplication
CC = Multiplication Property of Zero
DD = Multiplication Property of –1
EE = Substitution Property
FF = -4×-8
GG = Commutative Property of Addition
HH = Associative Property of Multiplication
II = Reflexive Property
JJ = $b + (4 + 5)$
KK = Multiplication Property of –1
LL = Distributive Property
MM = Substitution Property
NN = Distributive Property

Page 79

1. 5	6. –4	11. 7	16. –5	21. 17
2. 6	7. 2	12. –6	17. 8	22. 12
3. 9	8. 4	13. 11	18. –17	23. –11
4. –3	9. –2	14. –7	19. –13	24. –1
5. 1	10. 3	15. –8	20. 0	25. –20

Page 93

1. y^6	6. $2x^4$	11. x^{2a}	16. $81x^4y^{20}$	21. x^8
2. y^8	7. a^{10}	12. x^{a+2}	17. $81x^4y^{12}$	22. $6x^2y^2$
3. x^6y^9	8. a^7	13. $9a^6$	18. $4r^6b^2$	23. $9x^2y^2$
4. $8x^3$	9. y^{3x}	14. $27a^9$	19. $4r^4b^2$	24. x^6
5. $16x^4$	10. y^{4x}	15. b^5c^4	20. x^{15}	25. $16x^2$

Page 95 Top and bottom of a die when rolled will always equal seven (7).

Page 97

Type	*Measure*	*Type*	*Measure*	*Type*	*Measure*	*Type*	*Measure*
1. acute	58°	4. right	90°	7. obtuse	98°	10. obtuse	130°
2. straight	180°	5. acute	50°	8. acute	82°	11. straight	180°
3. acute	50°	6. acute	40°	9. right	90°	12. right	90°

Page 100

Puzzler 1 .... P = 10

Puzzler 2 .... P = 4

Puzzler 3 .... Each side of a square is equal in length. If one side measures 4, all other sides measure 4 as well.

Puzzler 4 .... Perimeter = 40

1. Easy Scramble

2. Simple Scramble

3. Scrample Lite

4. Cool Scramble

5. Triangle Teaser

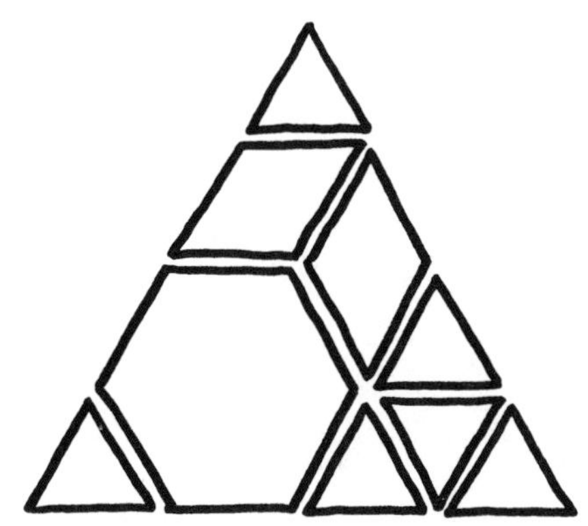

6. Triple Challenge

7. Super Scramble

Symmetry And More!

Step 1 On the line below each polygon, write the name of the shape (triangle, quadrilateral, pentagon, hexagon, octagon, or decagon).

Step 2 Draw all possible lines of symmetry on each of the polygons.

Step 3 Using the chart at the bottom of the page, list the polygons which contain specific lines of symmetry.

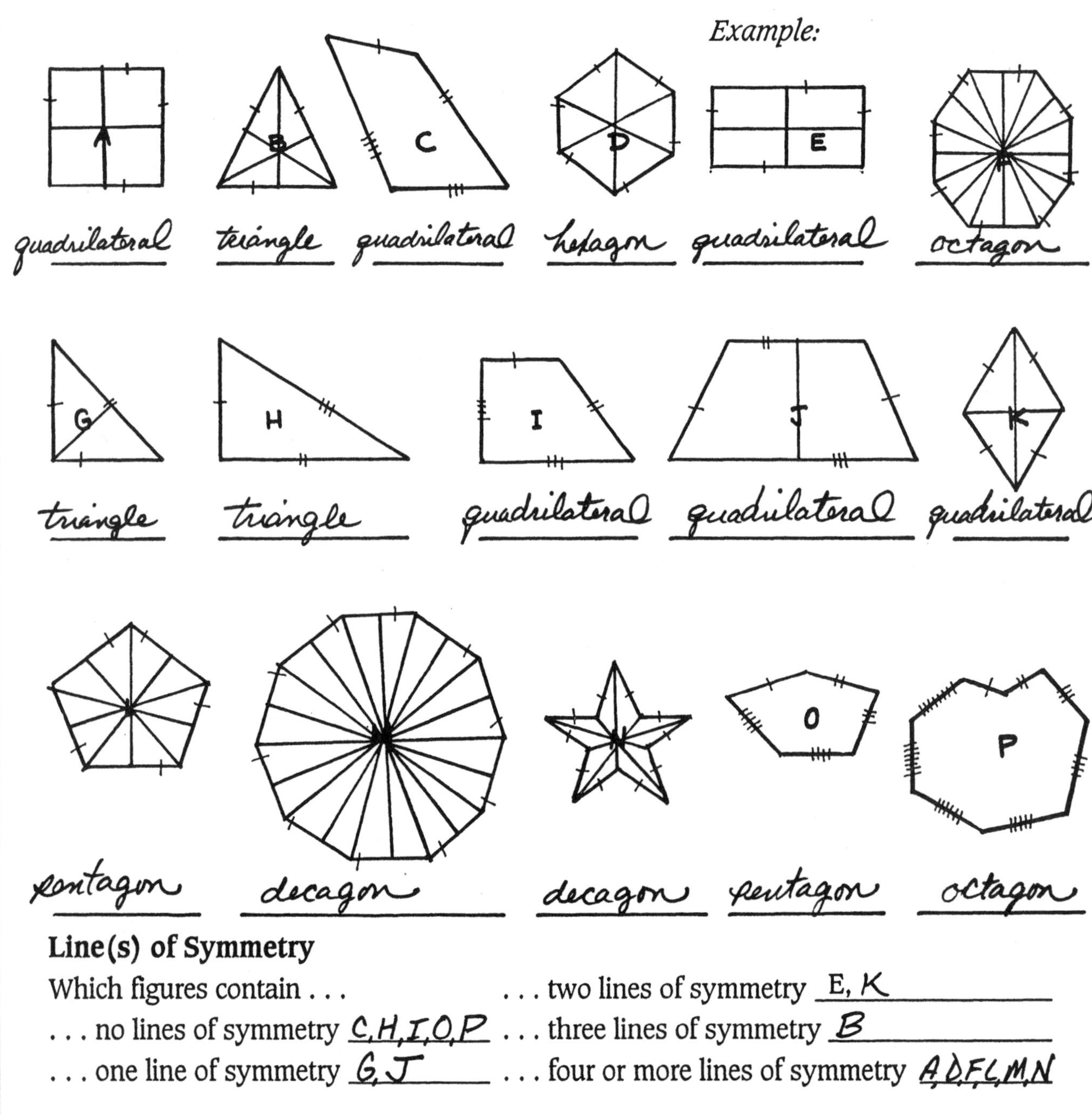

Line(s) of Symmetry

Which figures contain . . .

. . . no lines of symmetry C,H,I,O,P

. . . one line of symmetry G,J

. . . two lines of symmetry E, K

. . . three lines of symmetry B

. . . four or more lines of symmetry A,D,F,L,M,N